# Moral Ontology:

a thesis on the interdependence of sense, integrity and agency

**Michael Kowalik**

Michael Kowalik is an academically published philosopher writing on ethics, logic and theory of consciousness. Drawing on his formal model of reflexive consciousness, the author examines the causative relationship between logic, morality and conscious agency, which renders morality 'realist' in the sense that our actions have inescapable consequences for our capacities as agent. In addition to formulating an analytical framework for rationally solving complex moral dilemmas, the author defends the claim that the structure of sense, internalised as the logical consistency of Self-ideation with respect to other beings of the same kind, determines not only the moral integrity of our conduct but the ontological integrity of the Self, and that objective morality is not an impediment to conscious agency but its optimal realisation; the essence of creative power over meaning, which is the ultimate self-interest.

| | |
|---|---|
| Introduction | 1 |
| **Part One: Logic of Coexistence** | **9** |
| Theory of reflexive consciousness: the reality principle | 9 |
| Evolution of universal norms and transcendental authority | 26 |
| Ontological conditions of moral status | 44 |
| Logical consistency determines the integrity of conscious agency | 53 |
| **Part Two: Practical Ethics** | **63** |
| Prove your humanity | 63 |
| Discourse ethics | 67 |
| Golden Rule | 71 |
| Trolley Problem | 81 |
| Greater Good and Universal Rights | 84 |
| **Part Three: Rules of Meaning** | **93** |
| Law of identity | 93 |
| Hegel on identity by double-negation | 98 |
| The meaning of 1 | 101 |
| Law of non-contradiction and its relationship to identity and excluded middle | 104 |
| Principle of explosion | 107 |
| Principle of sufficient reason | 110 |
| Law of excluded middle | 111 |
| Rules of inference | 116 |
| Structure of knowledge | 122 |

# Introduction

The 'world as we know it' is governed by three fundamental laws: non-contradiction, excluded middle and identity. These laws are irrefutable and their authority is universal, since they are intrinsic to meaning, presupposed by the use of language or by intending to communicate and persuade. In order to contest their validity in a meaningful way, construct an argument that makes sense, one must obey them, thereby affirming their authority. A consistent refutation of the laws would implicitly validate its negation, therefore invalidate itself, and therefore would not be a consistent refutation of the laws. The three laws can be interpreted as different articulations of the same, fundamental principle: the 'principle of sense'. Sense is the absolute limit of meaning, of thought, it has not outside, hence the three laws are also referred to as the 'laws of thought'. To reject any of the laws is to render them all senseless, it therefore suffices to rely on the most intuitive formula, the law of non-contradiction, as the One law of meaning, the fundamental principle of knowledge, existence, action and value. Sense is the fundamental order.

You can either intend to do something or not intend to do it. A partial intention to act, which is distinct from an intention to act a part, is inconceivable, nonsensical. When you intend to 'make a statement about something' you can either make that statement or not make that statement; any partial statement about something amounts to not yet having made that statement (the law of excluded middle). Once you have made a statement about something it cannot be the case that you have not made that statement; the fact of having made the statement precludes the possibility of not having made that statement in the same situation and at the same time (the law of non-contradiction). When you make a statement about something, that something is distinct from every other thing; it is not any other thing but just the thing the statement is about, and this enduring identity of 'that something' is signified by the pronoun 'it' (the law of identity). If any of these conditions were not satisfied, the description of 'making a statement about something' would not make sense.

That you have already made and not yet made, and neither made nor not yet made that statement about something that is not that something... is non-sense. It amounts to conveying no information about possible facts or meaningful intentions. The statement taken as a whole is a series of words with no integrable or actionable meaning, unthinkable as a singular thought, inconceivable as an intention. Moreover, if the intended action is inconsistent with the aim that motivates the intention to act, the aim cannot be realised by means of that action; the action is said to be irrational, bound to fail, as in the case of having made and not having made a statement about something and or neither or both or not it, or pushing and pulling the same thing at the same time, at the same point and in the same direction. The resulting failure is contrary to our perceived self-interest and humans intuitively understand that they must avoid contradictory actions in order to reliably realise their aims. You cannot at the same time do and not do something, neither do nor not do that something, do it in whole by doing it only in part, or do something that is not that something. The laws of sense are paramount, the ultimate norm, the foundation of all truth; the three laws, their derivatives and practical implications are comprehensively discussed in the final chapter of this book.

Performative contradictions are uncontroversially self-defeating, but some situations may involve contradictory terms that are too complex for the agent to identify as contradictions. For example, does stealing or lying for personal gain entail a contradiction? Does it therefore ultimately lead to failure? Is intentional killing in self-defence a performative contradiction, acting against a deeper, more fundamental self-interest? These questions intentionally suggest a link between logic and ethics/morality, and render ethics and morality 'realist' in the sense that wrong intentions may have inescapable negative consequences for the agent. A further consideration is whether the negative moral consequences of action are tolerable for the sake of other valuable ends. For example, is gaining wealth through deception a good enough compensation for a conceptually remote metaphysical cost? Is national security maintained by intentionally killing the enemy combatants a good enough compensation for the associated metaphysical cost (if any)? Are we rationally justified in killing an innocent person to preserve the lives of many people (the trolley problem)? Does the majority have the right to kill an innocent minority to achieve a higher standard of public health? Does the end justify the means? If the end justifies the means then what justifies the end? In addition to formulating an analytical framework for rationally solving complex moral dilemmas, I argue that the structure of sense, internalised as the logical consistency of Self-ideation with respect to the world as we know it, determines not only the moral integrity of our conduct but the ontological integrity of Self, and that objective morality is not an impediment to agency but its optimal realisation, the essence of creative power over meaning, which is the ultimate self-interest.

Ethics is concerned with the distinction between right and wrong actions in relation to beings of the same kind - the essential rules of conduct that govern the social dimension. Morality is concerned with the distinction between right and wrong intentions - the essential rules that govern the propriety of the will in any context, and therefore includes ethics. The crucial link between moral knowledge and moral action, that which makes morality and ethics practically normative, consists in the weight of reasons to do what morality requires. The general desideratum of practical normativity is that it should allow the resolution of intersubjective conflicts by appealing to reasons that ought to be accepted as objective and universally motivating by all rational and sufficiently informed agents. In other words, rational moral norms must be fit to both guide and ground the circumstantially unique determinations about acting in a particular way.

The present work is premised on the theory of reflexive consciousness formulated in the paper 'Ontological-Transcendental Defence of Metanormative Realism' (Kowalik M. Philosophia, 2020), according to which subjective consciousness is, a priori, constitutively dependent on the consistency of reflexive relating with other beings of the same kind and on the systematic reciprocity of right intentions, grounded in rational self-interest. Morality, understood as 'principled discernment between right and wrong intentions', is therefore a constitutive property of conscious agency, thought and meaning. The degree of conscious agency, coextensive with the capacity to generate meaning, is determined by the logical consistency of our relating to all conscious agents.

Rational morality is grounded in what all rational agents

value about themselves: the capacity to generate meaning and bestow worth on things, actions and ideas. In order for this capacity to be consistently expressed at the social level we must respect it not only in ourselves but in everyone else, as a matter of principle. A meaningful existence is necessarily morally reflexive. In essence, we must act morally to preserve the integrity of the social dimension and a meaningful existence as integrated individuals. This is a crucial insight for ethics, as it presents us with an objective point of reference, a fundamental interest with respect to which we can qualify the value of specific actions. Moreover, knowing a priori that rational consciousness is not individually self-sufficient but requires reflexive social relations (type-mirroring) to conceive of itself and of the world, our relationship to other beings of the same kind is subject to a moral law that can be logically deduced.

The logical structure of rational consciousness is the basic norm of agency that can be reduced to two interdependent, provable, meta-moral facts: 1) rational agency values itself as the source of all meaning and contingent values - a fact that every agent affirms by choosing to act on a reason or valuing anything for a reason; 2) the integrity of rational agency is a function of reflexive relating with conscious others. It follows from (2) that non-compliance with the basic norm results in incremental dis-integration of Self, therefore in a lower degree of reflexive consciousness and in a diminished capacity to generate meaning, which is contrary to self-interest (1).

Reflexive consciousness is integrated with objective reality in a special way. The classical view that the noumenon (reality as 'thing-in-itself') can inform us about object-identities within it, or about its all-encompassing-being, implies that there are 'real' conceptual boundaries or identity distinctions (concepts) that pre-exist the conceptual boundaries and identity-distinctions that arise in our minds, and that we discover or infer or intuit or otherwise represent those *original* concepts on the basis of experience. An alternative view is that all boundaries and identity distinctions are generated by consciousness, 'in' consciousness, to 'fit' consciousness, and we conceptually integrate them in a way that reliably differentiates between objective reality and subjective experience as sub-domains of meaning. Only the latter view avoids the circular logic of positing 'the world as we know it' (meaningful and knowable as an object of thought, a concept 'in the mind') as an identity that exists also independently of the concept in the mind, but is still thought of and perceived as just *that* concept. A consistent idea of 'the world as we know it' is synonymous with 'objective reality', insofar as what we identify as the world is causally and intersubjectively integrated.

Since consciousness encompasses every theory and concept, including the concept of time, the theory of consciousness does not need to accommodate a non-conscious source or beginning. The primary explanatory challenge associated with this world-model is that reflexive consciousness is logically self-referential, which entails logical circularity, but it does not lead to contradiction provided that the self-reference is mediated by another term, in the sense of mutual mirroring. Consciousness can be consistently modelled only in terms of a reflexive multiplicity, which is a universal, structural constraint that provides the ontological basis for moral norms.

It is tautologically and therefore trivially true that we cannot know anything apart from the world 'as we know it'. It is logically and non-trivially true that we cannot know anything apart from the world as 'we' (a multiplicity of beings of the same ontological kind) know it. In this sense, the reflexive multiplicity entailed by rational consciousness is the generative principle of the world, a world that could not exist without consciousness because it is a world only insofar as it is meaningful, and meaning is structurally limited by the laws of sense. We can entertain and believe a lot of nonsense, harbour many contradictions, but this only means that some of our beliefs are false, that they do not correspond to objects in the world as we know it, not even to objects in our imagination, but are only poorly constructed expressions that signify nothing apart from their inconsistent parts. We may signify a contradictory description with a name, but we cannot imagine that alleged something as a meaningful identity; it is a cluster of words that do not make up a meaningful whole. A contradictory 'identity' is ineffable, therefore not an identity but a void in the relational structure of meaning, a void in the world as we know it, not real. Objective reality is a special sub-domain of sense.

Meaning is coextensive with what we know as existence, as reality, as time, as culture, and as science; a product of socially mediated rational consciousness, which by virtue of its reflexive structure entails creative power over the conditions of existence, a kind of power that continuously modulates reality, guides it towards new possibilities of meaning-as-being, and augments the terms of causal integration. Rational consciousness and, by implication, rational morality, transcend the utility of deception and violence, which are subject to the contemporaneous conditions of existence, causally deterministic and ultimately self-defeating insofar as they are inconsistent with the logical structure of the Self, causing its dis-integration.

It is evident that ideological proclamations of universal love, cosmic interdependence, human brotherhood and loving our enemies failed to persuade, as the contemporary society is still afflicted by irreconcilable disagreements and violence that plagued the ancient world. If morality is not persuasive to those who benefit from immorality, then why be moral? People cannot be persuaded by moral teachings that are contrary to their interest. Moral theory *must* be persuasive, and in order to be persuasive it *must* appeal to verifiable, rational self-interest, above all else, and until that happens every proclamation of human unity and common interest, every political system or ideology, will be perverted and inverted, reduced to the lowest common denominator, which is irrationality and violence.

I argue that there are meta-moral facts that can be proven a priori, as provisionally outlined above, that from these facts we can derive the objective distinction between right and wrong intentions in various practical circumstances, and that it serves our interest to do so.

# Part One: Logic of Coexistence

## Theory of reflexive consciousness: the reality principle

The sense of becoming 'more conscious' or developing 'more agency' is, for the most part, counterintuitive and analytically unexplored. In this section I consider my previously published model of conscious agency, which incorporates degrees of reflexive consciousness and the function of their determination in relation to the world as we know it, with the aim of formulating a logically consistent, meta-moral ontology. This extended account of reflexive consciousness will explain the sense of what it is like for the degree of reflexive consciousness to change as a consequence of social relations.

I provisionally employ the term 'reflexive consciousness' to signify the capacity to identify instances of meaning/sense (ideas) as belonging to a temporally continuous, singular identity, and to have higher-order ideas about ideas. I use the term 'thought' to signify the instances of identification of meaning/sense as belonging to a temporally continuous, singular identity. The ideas signified by the terms self, other, inside, outside, perception, time, world, nature, body, feeling, idea, signifier and signified are examples of meaningful objects of thought. By invoking these signifiers (tokens of meaning) we identify what they mean in terms of other ideas, including their higher order meanings as members of categories and as words, tokens or signifiers. All tokens of meaning are systemically cross-referential, that is, they can be defined only in terms of other tokens of meaning. It is impossible for consciousness to intentionally evade thought, as any intentional reference to non-thought is already a distinction in thought, an act of thinking about thoughts as objects in the relational structure of meaning. On this view, everything meaningful constitutes an integrated object of though, an identifiable set of relations that can be grasped by reflexive consciousness all at once, as a higher order unity of sense. Mutually exclusive meanings cannot be expressed in the same thought, nor can they be simultaneously intended for action, and it is impossible to think a thought that both affirms and denies the same meaning (the law of non-contradiction). A statement that affirms and denies the same meaning has no meaning beyond the incompatibility of its parts, which are two successive thoughts of which one must be denied for the other to be meaningful. Another way, "if a proposition has no sense, nothing corresponds to it, since it does not designate a thing (a truth-value) which might have properties called 'false' or 'true'." (Wittgenstein, Ludwig. Tractatus Logico-Philosophicus. Routledge & Kegan Paul, 1974, 4.063)

The content of reflexive consciousness is intrinsically ordered according to logical types - different positions in the hierarchy of relations (if X is about Y and Y is about Z then Z is not about Y and Y is not about X, unless X is Y is Z) - and is meaningful only because it is differentiated by type. A meaningful idea consists in its difference from everything else (the law of identity), including the difference of logical type. Crucially, individual thought is constitutively dependent on multiple loci of 'other' consciousness that are unique in their individualised apprehension of 'the same' meaning. To apprehend meaning is to consistently identify an object of thought as meaningful to other beings of the same kind in the same situation; a first person perspective on a property held in common, where the sense of commonality grounds the perspective 'on something already there' and the meaning of the property consists in the commonality of its sense, or what the property 'is like' to me and to others, and therefore 'true'. Consciousness can exist as an integrated, higher-order idea only socially, as a reflexive multiplicity.

The intersubjective domain of meaning is akin to the phenomenological surplus arising between imperfect mirrors facing one another, reflecting but also distorting the reflection. In the objective sense, nothing extra is added to the situation and yet infinite depth is created, an infinite potential for content, which is both internal to each mirror and external, reproduced in one another. The structure of consciousness is like the double-mirror effect that transcends the interiority of meaning, its subjectivity, by means of reflexive entanglement between multiple subjects that sustains every instance of meaning and being as something held both in common and also individually, characterised as something 'out there' and 'for me'. The world is individually external but collectively internal, objectified via imperfect reflexive correspondence between instances of awareness: the meaning of being as that which is identical to being 'in itself'.

Within the reflexive space of awareness, infinite articulations of meaning are possible. The essential function of rational consciousness is to continuously re-contextualise the reflected sense in relation to the infinite potential for objectifying the content, as a new part of reality, in logical continuity with the past, and to filter out non-sense, which has no integrated meaning, no identity, therefore no existence. Original ideas can then be consistently synthesised from the reflected instances of sense without disrupting the relational integrity of the meaning held in common.

At the limit of the intersubjective synthesis of meaning is the natural world. Nature can be characterised as a manifestation of the collective unconscious, the totality of meanings that consciousness progressively externalised as having the relational integrity of a causally closed, deterministic system. Another way, the natural world is the externalised record of the contingencies arising in the evolution of meaning, our collective memory, which can be recalled via direct awareness of meaningful phenomena. Behind this process is the structure that organises the creation of the world via the rules of discernment of possible vs. impossible, real vs. unreal, true vs. false, sense vs. nonsense, in every social manifestation of rational consciousness. As such, the world is meaning, every real part of which is meaningful and contemporaneously necessary to sustain the conceptual integrity and the narrative continuity of phenomena, making the world existentially conditional on reflexive consciousness. The principle of sense is above and before the world, the ultimate reality, it is also represented in the world as embodied consciousness, capable of thought and language, and it is the world as its meaningful appearance and experience.

Every aspect of nature is an idea, a concept, a meaning; otherwise it would not be meaningful to consciousness as a phenomenon or as a sensation with particular characteristics, therefore not discernible as anything at all. The ideas comprising the natural world were generated by the interacting, logically entangled loci of consciousness, from the beginning of time and including the concept of time. It follows that nature is a projection of the most ontologically inert constructs of rational consciousness. We depend on these constructs to ground ourselves as individual minds vis-a-vis one another in the same world of relations, and by reflecting on the logical structure of the world we become conscious of consciousness itself being the creator of meaning-as-being. This is what I mean by consciousness transcending nature.

The prevailing (classical) view is that rational consciousness emerged from the natural world, deemed to be a necessary condition of consciousness, and subsequently made it meaningful for itself, which now allows us to posit the idea of physical reality whose history predates consciousness and the associated ideas. This is true for the present only insofar as consciousness has the capacity to retroactively synthesise the chronology of its own evolution from the contemporaneous meaning-content that has the status of reality - a narrative about the past embedded within the narrative about the present - but it fails to consistently account for the logical type distinction between the order of changes in reality and the order of changes in the idea of reality. If the necessary pre-conditions of consciousness are real only insofar as they are meaningful, which implies objects of thought whose meaning is just what those pre-conditions of consciousness are, then the pre-conditions of consciousness are conditional on the consequent states of consciousness, therefore the condition is its own conditional, the cause is its own effect, *causa sui*, therefore non-sense. The two causative orders of consciousness and objective reality cannot be logically integrated on the same dimension.

Reflexive consciousness is self-evident, but it would not suffice to assert that both thought and the reality signified by thought occur on the same temporal dimension: the causal sequence of ideas. This would account for the direction and order of the evolution of ideas, as objects of thought, but the sense of having ideas, their meaning, is precisely that they signify something more than thoughts, a correlate to consciousness that grounds the distinction between the idea of objective reality and the subjectivity of thought. Conversely, the strictly physicalist view, according to which consciousness and the rules of sense are just a manifestation of noumenal reality whose existence is independent of consciousness, therefore consciousness and the rules of sense are not necessary to existence, does not work either. It implies that objective reality is 'in itself' meaningless, senseless, therefore nothing in particular or in general, which contradicts the premise that it exists or is real and undergoes change, let alone that it can be experienced or known in its particulars, or that descriptions of its particulars can be either true or false. Alternatively, the physicalist view renders meaning and sense inexplicable, assumed without sufficient reason, therefore everything is inexplicable, including the physical. It is also immaterial whether what we call 'objective reality' is wholly independent of consciousness or whether it is composed only of ideas that are grounded in a special way; the distinction between objectivity and subjectivity implies that individual consciousness is at least in part distinct from objective reality but is also a necessary condition of its objectivity, insofar as it makes it meaningful as 'what' it is.

The ontological duality of subjective consciousness and objective reality implies that the real thing and the idea of the thing can both change in time, at least in part independently of one another. Real things uncontroversially change in time, they change in their constitution, not in their identity, but the idea of a thing can also change when we conceive of something about things that we did not conceive of before, and this newly conceived of property necessitates (as a matter of systemic consistency) a new idea of what that thing always was and how it 'really' related to other things in the past. In effect, a new historical identity of a thing retroactively replaces the former identity. The implicit ontological commitment associated with this substitution is that the new historical identity of the thing is true, therefore it 'is' the thing of the past, and the former identity is false, therefore it 'is not' and 'was not' the thing of the past. This intuitively makes sense because a thing can have only one true identity at a time, but if the past identity of a thing is not the same as the present identity, then we have not merely changed our idea of what a particular thing always was but identified different things; things that are logically related in a special way, insofar as one 'takes the place' of the other or belongs in a different 'possible world', but they are nevertheless different things. This result is entailed by the law of non-contradiction; the past identity cannot be the present identity if the former is false and the latter is true, nor can a false identity that never existed 'become' a true identity than now exists (the law of identity). Another way, a thing that exists necessarily endures in time, therefore has to be identified as the same thing at different times despite any changes in its constitution, but because we conceptualise things differently at different times then the meaning and therefore the identity of a thing that once was is distinct from what it is now, therefore the same identity is not the same identity, therefore contradiction. A contradictory theory of temporal identity cannot be true.

Since we can identify reality only in terms of ideas/concepts, which are instances of meaning, the idea/concept of the pre-conditions of thought and its meaning as the 'real' pre-conditions of thought can be neither fully disentangled nor equated; despite being different logical types of objects, they are conceptually indispensable aspects of the same, ontologically continuous being. The concept, an object of though, defines the identifying characteristics of something other than itself, which is nevertheless nothing (has no identity) apart from that concept. To consistently accommodate this inherent sense-duality requires two-dimensional time (Kowalik M. Two-dimensional time. Pre-print, 2020), or more specifically, two atemporal dimensions that only together constitute time and their intersection is the present, coincidental with the state of reflexive consciousness. On the first dimension, reality undergoes a series of constitutive transformations, whereas the present meaning/identity of an object is attributed to multiple constitutive states in that series. This is how we think about the history of changes in commonly identified objects; by retroactively projecting their present meaning/identity. On the second dimension, reality is constitutively fixed insofar as it is 'the present' for our perception, whereas the meaning of what is perceived in the present ideational context is differentiated from the meaning of similar perceptions in former ideational contexts. This is how we think about relations and properties that characterise the evolving meaning/identity of what we perceive; by retroactively projecting the present state of awareness. The two types of temporal ideation are logically compatible and integrable with reflexive consciousness. The present identity is contextualised and consequently augmented by a series of perceptions of reality, whereas the present perception of reality is contextualised and consequently augmented by a series of identity transformations. The present state of awareness contextualises the transformations of meaning, and the present state of meaning contextualises the transformations of awareness. This process is non-deterministic and ontologically generative.

A hypothetical world fashioned on the ontological commitments of strict, temporally-linear realism, consisting of immutable identities that exist 'in themselves' and are independent of consciousness, is ontologically complete and deterministic... and false. Every change in an ontologically complete world is a constitutive feature and therefore continuation of its temporally fixed ontology; not a change of identity, not a beginning, not originality, but consequences and repetition. "A singularity is that with which a thought begins. But if this beginning is a mere consequence of the logical laws of a world, it merely appears in its place and begins - strictly speaking - nothing." (Badiou, Alain. Logics of Worlds: Being and Event II. Continuum, 2009, 357) A world based on strictly physicalist, extrinsic criteria cannot be the real world; it excludes the domain of reflexive consciousness that cannot be totalised and is therefore ontologically incomplete, and without consciousness the world is meaningless, senseless, without identity, without differences or boundaries, therefore nothing. Conversely, consciousness can only conceive of 'the world as we know it', which is essentially incomplete in regard to the infinite possibilities of description in terms of identities and relations.

Ontological incompleteness entails temporal incompleteness of identity, which necessitates the creation of explanatory and justificatory reasons to sustain the continuity of sense. When perceiving change, we generate meaning that augments the identity that nominally endures through change. Change implies a plurality of constitutive states that are not only ordered sequentially in terms of 'before' and 'after' but partake in the ontological continuity *from* the state before *to* the state after. That x is before y expresses only a sequence of discrete states of being; it does not entail that x *becomes* y, let alone that x *is* y. Different states of being are not the same identity unless a special relationship is maintained between them. Ontological continuity from *before* to *after* is maintained only when the identity x+Δx takes the place of the former identity x, but also preserves x as a logical point of reference for the substitution. The content of change (Δx), the pure difference between two constitutive states of 'the same' reality, was not real prior to the change of identity and it is not a logical consequence of x, but something original. Once realised, it cannot be erased from the history of meaning. This, we can say, is the sense of the consciousness of change. Ontological incompleteness is a structural imbalance that moves consciousness to pursue incremental completion vis-a-vis the unknown, which is the indeterminate 'future' of thought, which is reason, which is the generative intentionality of conscious agency.

The identity of enduring objects is based on episodic awareness, centred on phenomenological features that make multiple episodes consistently distinguishable as the same type of experience, despite each episode being phenomenologically unique. When we identify two unique episodes of awareness as being 'the same' we do not mean that they are identical in every respect, not that they are 'one and the same' episode of awareness, but have the relation of identity restricted to type. "When one says 'x is identical with y,' this, I hold, is an incomplete expression; it is short for 'x is the same A as y' where 'A' represents some count noun understood from the context of utterance - or else, it is just a vague expression of a half-formed thought." (Geach, Peter Thomas. Identity. The Review of Metaphysics, 1967).

Another way, instances of awareness are phenomenologically unique, different, therefore not identical, and cannot be identified without referring to other instances of awareness that are alike and associating them by type vis-a-vis other types, which is an ontologically incomplete, reflexive process analogous to consciousness (this analogy will be formalised in the following pages).

At a higher lever of abstraction, identity presupposes narrative continuity and coherence with other identities. The Ship of Theseus, for example, retains its historical identity after total reconstitution insofar as it has functional continuity for the individuals who use it and can be phenomenologically distinguished from every other ship, but the reconstituted ship is not 'necessarily' the same identity as the original; a different historical narrative and different phenomenological features could have been functionally prioritised. The distinction between identities is essentially ideational, narrative, but also systemic; all identities in a world are mutually constraining insofar as they must be relationally consistent in order to make sense as objects in the same world. Narrative coherence of a world necessitates that all object-identities change relative to one another, change as a world, because they are ontologically co-dependent as limits for other identities.

The identity of conscious agents is narratively centred on individual bodies, which are objects that mediate intentional action in a world, but this does not exhaust the sense of conscious identity. Reflexive consciousness is characterised by identifying multiple episodes of awareness as belonging to the same stream of awareness, which can be identified in higher-order episodes of awareness within that stream. Moreover, the concept of the stream of awareness presupposes a common, temporally continuous locus in all the episodes of awareness, which under reflexive scrutiny is identified as the Self. From the perspective of consciousness, the body is internal to consciousness, a narrative representation of the Self in objective reality. From the position of the body, consciousness is internal to the body, a narrative representation of itself. As I argued above, the dual sense of conscious identity, both objective and subjective, physical and metaphysical, thing and idea, necessitates two-dimensional time to maintain narrative coherence. Both dimensions are necessary for a coherent conception of world/reality, but it can be shown that only one of the two domains is ontologically fundamental, while the other is complementary. Reflexive consciousness presupposes and includes the awareness of its narrative and ontological continuity, centred on the same locus of consciousness, which is the same and only coherent Self possible, despite any differences between episodes of awareness and states of consciousness at different times, and despite the changing conceptions of self-identity. This is not the case for the constitutive states of the body, which differ at different times but lack the narrative and ontological continuity apart from that imposed by conscious ideation. It follows that there can be no continuity of being, no world, without a subject 'of the situation' with whom to associate different states of being under the same identity. Consciousness grounds the temporal continuity of the body, and as such also grounds temporality. We must therefore conclude that reflexive consciousness, insofar as it is possible only vis-a-vis other conscious agents of the same kind experiencing each other subjectively, and insofar as it is conditional on the objectivity of 'the world as we know it' mediating the intersubjective relations, is an intrinsically two-dimensional process of identity-formation.

The story of the emergence of reflexive consciousness as a multiplicity of beings of the same kind is not yet logically complete. It would be impossible for two autonomous, conscious beings to understand one another, to agree on the meaning of experiences, symbols or words without already having something meaningful in common, so the resulting understanding could be an extension of the intrinsic commonality. We would not know whether we are in agreement about what anything 'is like' unless we already shared the conditions of agreement. It follows that when we perceive the world as something external we are also referring to something internal to our being that is held in common, socially, and makes the external mutually meaningful and true. The world 'out there' is meaningful to us individually as an externality only because it is already internal to our kind, already conceptual, linguistic, a world-model generated and maintained by reciprocal interaction with other members of the kind rather than independently discovered, internally reconstructed in a unique (subjective) way and then inexplicably communicated and understood by others. In this sense, all existence is reflexively evolved, generated and set in motion by a network of individually distributed instances of the same kind of consciousness, reflected in other instances of analogous structure. The subsequent states of the totality of existence are a consequence of its inherent motion and continuous augmentation by consciousness mirroring itself as a multiplicity. Consciousness grounds the world as we know it via reflexive multiplicity.

In the article Ontological-Transcendental Defence of Metanormative Realism (Philosophia, 2020) I argued that direct (monadic) self-awareness is logically impossible and presented a formal model of conscious agency based on indirect, socially mediated self-ideation, involving the synthesis of individual identity and the common identity of an ontological kind.

To briefly rehash the preliminary argument, monadic consciousness is logically impossible because direct self-reference either collapses to pure self-identity, which is trivially true of everything but does not entail reflexive consciousness, or presupposes itself as something 'meaningful', which is in excess of self-identity, as a concept of itself constructed in terms of itself and contained within itself, therefore is both identical and not identical to itself, therefore either a contradiction or no reflexive consciousness. This conclusion can be made more salient by the analogy of a sentence that refers to itself: 'This sentence is true'. The law of identity is implicitly violated by equivocating between the identity of the sentence 'This sentence is true' and the word 'sentence' in the sentence. It can be demonstrated that these two instances of 'sentence' are not the same identity. In fact, the phrase 'This sentence' does not refer to anything at all: substitution of the whole sentence for every recurrent instance of the phrase 'This sentence' results in infinite regress and an empty subject: "(((((...) is true) is true) is true)...)". The sentence cannot be meaningfully completed; when consistently parsed it does not make sense and is not even a sentence. Another way, a monadic self implies no image or sense of 'what' it is.

An individual cannot meaningfully relate to self all by itself or by means of relations between its parts. Self-identification as an individual requires something other than self to characterise the content of identity in terms of what it is 'like', or else it is nothing. Reflexive consciousness identifies the constant of its narrative continuity (the subject) as an object that is phenomenologically identifiable only in relation to other objects of the same kind. When I recognise my face in the mirror, or simply think about myself, I implicitly identify as a member of a particular kind of beings that makes my identity meaningful as an individual of *that* kind.

We exist as conscious individuals vis-a-vis other beings of the same kind, whose self-recognition as conscious individuals hinges on commonality and reciprocity of meaning. The logic of socially mediated self-reference can be formalised as the axiom of subjectivity: an individual **a** is reflexively conscious only if **a** relates to itself by relating to a different individual **b** that relates to itself by relating to **a**, in terms of properties **f** common to them both, and **a** is not identical to **b**. In the following diagram it is assumed that reflexive relations between **a** and **b** are perfectly consistent (**a** identifies with **f** in **b** as much as **f** in **a**, and **b** identifies with **f** in **a** as much as **f** in **b**), which implies that **a** and **b** are mutually integrated selves, with the maximum degree of relative existence as conscious agents. Any inconsistency in identifying with **f** in another would entail a reflexive inconsistency in oneself, an incomplete self-reference, therefore a meaningless void or a disassociation in self-identity, resulting in a lower degree of reflexive consciousness. The present model is limited to two individuals (**a** and **b**), but any number of individuals (a multiplicity) can and do maintain reflexive relations by means of a common part. The range of meaning held in common includes (the meaning of) common reality, and the common reality includes (the meaning of) common embodiment ($\mathbf{f} \supset \mathbf{R} \supset \mathbf{n}$).

## Reflexive Consciousness

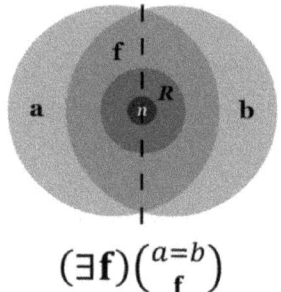

**f**: common meaning
**R**: common reality in **f**
**n**: common embodiment in **R**
**a, b**: spheres of subjectivity

$$(\exists f)\binom{a=b}{f}$$

The 'commonality' of meaning entails that it is a property of multiple individuals, grounded in the logical and temporal continuity of its socially-mediated construction, and is therefore an objective, normative property that individual agents are constitutively subject to. For example, to deny the sense of language to another is to implicitly corrupt the sense of language for oneself and thereby diminish one's own capacity to make sense and generate common meaning. To deny the reflexive consciousness of another, who is constituted as such via reflexive relating with the multiplicity of conscious others, is to disrupt one's own reflexive relating with the grounding multiplicity and thus become less conscious as an agent. To deny the sense of language to a group of individuals, constituted as conscious agents via reflexive relating with the multiplicity, but retain the sense of language for another group of conscious agents in the same language-community, is to disrupt one's own reflexive relating with the grounding multiplicity and thus become less conscious, less integrated as an agent, with less creative power over meaning and the associated conditions of existence (**R**, **n**).

The scope of the meaning-content can nevertheless vary between communication-communities, potentially ranging from the basic survival/sexual co-dependency to complex systemic abstractions. In the hierarchy of reflexive orders, the common embodiment is a grounding condition for the more abstract orders of commonality. In the case of non-reflexive awareness among individuals of the same kind, **f** and **R** are coextensive with and thus limited to the awareness of common embodiment.

**Non-Reflexive Awareness**

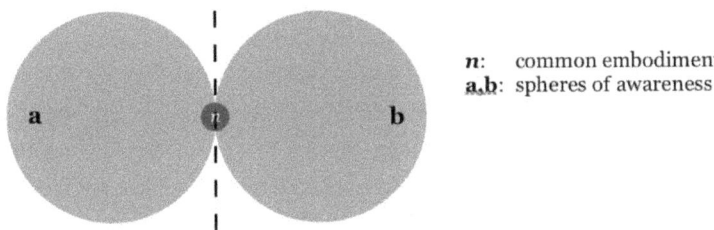

$n$: common embodiment
$a, b$: spheres of awareness

It follows from the above formulation that reflexive consciousness could not be generated apart from the evolution of an embodied community. Consciousness is coextensive with meaning, the fundamental order, which is socially generated via countless transformations of antecedent meanings, and as such requires conceptual continuity from the non-reflexive state of episodic awareness, which must be regarded as the minimal state of individuation. Consciousness co-evolves its own world and embodiment, which precludes any artificial or constructed, or alien, or monadic/non-social consciousness manifesting itself or existing in the same world. Nevertheless, to avoid infinite regress, there must be something irreducible and atemporal about consciousness for it to have generated a world for itself and 'become' reflexive in that world.

A conscious individual could not recognise another conscious individual as a conscious individual without sensing their point of contact and reflexive consciousness as something already held in common. It follows that consciousness of different individuals is not wholly individual but in part identical and therefore, by the law of identity, not fully encoded in the physically separate, individual bodies. It necessarily depends on something universal; an ontological essence. Since reflexive consciousness had to be co-evolved with the objective reality that mediates reflexive relations, the social connection must be meaningfully encoded and manifested in that reality, whereby multiple loci of consciousness can directly sense one another as beings of the same kind. Irrespective of the mechanism involved, we sense others as instances of ourselves, biologically autonomous but sharing the same essence, internally differentiated and contextually individualised, and only in this social cloud the sense of individuality exists, as a constitutive element of the ontological kind. The degree of consciousness is determined by the consistency of reflexive relating with other rational beings in terms of properties common to them all, evolved via embodied socialisation. This is the ontological basis of objective morality.

## Evolution of universal norms and transcendental authority

Reflexive consciousness is characterised by the idea that multiple episodes of awareness belong to the same stream of awareness and can be selectively identified, represented and synthesised into higher-order episodes of awareness within that stream. Moreover, the concept of the stream of awareness presupposes a singular, temporally continuous locus in all the episodes of awareness, which is identified as the Self (I) by identifying with other selves in terms of common properties.

The emergence of reflexive consciousness is etiologically inconceivable without being preceded by the non-reflexive (animal) awareness of the distinction between frequently repeated episodes and sporadic episodes, generalised as the sense of familiarity and strangeness. The most essential, existentially relevant type of episodic repetition for every species is their interaction with other members of the same species. The locus of episodic awareness is thus anchored in the existentially indispensable ideation of one's own ontological kind.

The scope of animal ideation of the species is typically limited to the reproductive function and to physical dominance, but at some point in the evolution of awareness a new mode of identity emerged, based on unique patterns of intentionality expressed by individuals vis-a-vis one another: the face. Faces are directional, intrinsically outward-facing, other-facing, reflection-facing, and thus phenomenologically blind to themselves without external, reflexive mediation. Early human ancestors could not have conceived of their own faces until they conceived of the face of another and thus began to conceive of themselves in terms of another. This reflexive turn marked the beginning of conscious self-ideation, which is nevertheless always only indirect, mediated by the phenomenological ideation of others. Self-identity is the conceptual synthesis of others from first-person perspective, a mental act of internalising other beings of the same kind as my-Self in a situation.

Phenomenologically, our sense of Self is grounded in the reflexivity of face-to-face relations. We can identify as I, as Self, only in terms of what we identify with, and we can meaningfully 'identify with' only in terms of what we perceive to be a-like. We are the likeness of Man, the universal face in which we recognise our humanity as the humanity of others. The ancient concept of *anthropos*, 'one who is alike', 'of human likeness', is not just a historical artefact but a profound, metaphysical insight. Unless I can compare my human-likeness to the likeness of another there is literally nothing *like* being me, because 'being me' entails the awareness that I am like someone else. The logical impossibility of direct (monadic) self-ideation, which can only be fulfilled via reflexive mirroring with other beings of the same kind, face-to-face, is the ontological foundation of language. The face is the universal 'first language'.

"Directness of the face-to-face, a 'between us', already conversation, already dialogue and hence distance and quite the opposite of the contact in which coincidence and identification occur. But this is precisely the distance of proximity, the marvel of the social relation. In that relation, the difference between the I and the other remains. But it is maintained as the denial, in proximity which is also difference, of its own negation, as non-in-difference toward one another. Like the non-indifference between close friends or relatives. Being concerned by the alterity of the other: fraternity." (Levinas, Emmanuel. Alterity and Transcendence. The Athlone Press, 1999, 93-94)

Your face is that which speaks to me, that sees me, that sees me respond to you and therefore responds; all these modes of reflexive communication occur simultaneously, in one embodiment, phenomenologically unified and individualised for me as another Self. Conversely, my face speaks to others, sees the faces of others focussed on my face and responds to them. If these signals were disjointed, emanated without a face, there would be no phenomenological unity to the distinct modes of information, no narrative continuity, no personhood. Ultimately, the face itself communicates, non-verbally, visually; it conveys the presence and attention of another conscious agency and the ontological characteristics that make us alike but not identical vis-a-vis one another. This reflexive recognition is perhaps detected subconsciously, as an instantaneous bond that we may honour and thus be true to kind, or violate and thus negate our kind and, implicitly, negate our own identity.

From the axiom of subjectivity: the more faithfully we integrate our kind as the ground of self-ideation the more integrated and conscious we became as agents. Our intentions become more consistent with the generative, reflexive structure of socially-mediated consciousness and we thus acquire more creative power over meaning, language and reality. Conversely, by alienating ourselves from our kind we disrupt the conditions of reflexive consciousness, degrade the sense of speech and reality, and incrementally disintegrate as conscious agents. The resulting regression to deterministic, compulsive, unconscious behaviour also marginally disrupts the integrity of our kind, facilitating catastrophic consequences for the self-alienating individual and harm to others.

The meaning of human history consists in the unceasing struggle to understand and manage the social consequences of individual action. The oldest framework for normalising social relations of can be characterised as tribalism, whose central normative feature was moral allegiance on the basis of blood-relations within a particular territory, mediated by idiosyncratic mythologies of the sacred. "In general it can be said that myth, as experienced by archaic societies, (1) constitutes the History of the acts of the Supernaturals; (2) that this History is considered to be absolutely *true* (because it is concerned with realities) and *sacred* (because it is the work of the Supernaturals; (3) that myth is always related to a 'creation,' it tells how something came into existence, or how a pattern of behaviour, an institution, a manner of working were established; this is why myths constitute the paradigms for all significant human acts; (4) that by knowing the myth one knows the 'origin' of thing and hence can control and manipulate them at will; this is not an 'external,' 'abstract' knowledge but a knowledge that one 'experiences' ritually, either by ceremonially recounting the myth or by performing the ritual for which it is the justification; (5) that in one way or another one 'lives' the myth, in the sense that one is seized bythe sacred, exalting power of the events recollected or re-enacted." (Eliade, Mircea. Myth and Reality. Harper & Row, 1963, 18-19)

Due to the idiosyncratic group-ideation that characterised archaic societies, the tribal mindset was inherently clan-centric and antagonistic to those who did not share its ritual knowledge of the sacred and therefore could never 'belong' in their native habitat, which was the substance of that knowledge. It generally considered harmful acts done to outsiders by members of the tribe as less wrong or less deserving of restitution than the same acts done to members of the tribe by outsiders, implicitly or explicitly ascribing a higher moral status to one's own group-identity. It is not without significance that the term Eco is derived from the Greek word *oîkos*, meaning *home*. The natives are, by virtue of their supernatural endowment, in their natural, original and therefore sacred home, whereas non-natives are profane outsiders, trespassers against the supernatural and an irredeemable threat to the sacred balance of existence, a moral wrong that has to be suppressed or eliminated in order to maintain the mythical order.

It is trivially true that every human is a product of their ancestors and their cumulative experiences, but tribal ethics devalued or did not conceive of the fact that we all share the same ancestors, that we are all related, and instead carved out an arbitrary but morally absolute value-distinction in a particular time and place. Nevertheless, the injustice of tribalism is not the emphasis on bloodline in the construction of personal identity and moral status, but the implicit devaluation of the fact that the significance of bloodline is still logically subordinate to our common capacity to generate meaning with one another.

The primary function of tribal ethics was evidently to preserve the integrity of its space-bound, mythical group-ideation and thus maintain the power to reliably fulfil the common aim of survival within the native territory. Despite superior group cohesion, the stronger positive emphasis on identification with the tribe than with humanity was the limiting condition of tribal self-ideation and power. Frequent interactions between tribes required a new kind of skill that the inherently insular tribal cultures did not possess: to resolve conflicting beliefs and reach understanding on the basis of what the interacting tribes had in common. The ability to transcend bloodlines and idiosyncratic mythologies, and socially integrate at a higher conceptual level was positively associated with economic and military power, allowing multi-tribal nations to colonise tribal territories and coercively absorb their members.

"The Greeks were probably the first culture to develop an image of the human not primarily as a member of this race of tribe or of that, but as an individual being." (Markley, O.W. Changing Images of Man. Pergamon Press, 1982, 25)

The emerging civilisations and empires consisted of groups that were able to bridge the gaps in meaning between tribal narratives and submit to a common social order. By transgressing tribal boundaries, disrupting the indigenous, place-bound communities that were culturally inert and insular, colonisation stimulated conceptual evolution and transcendence, initially via religious syncretism and later advancing towards human integration as a universal kind of rational beings, beyond tribal and religious identities. The interacting cultures were mutually contextualised, their insular traditions relativised, their symbols reinterpreted, their inconsistencies and social conditioning reciprocally challenged, compelling both the coloniser and the colonised to deliberate, come to terms, and ultimately affirm what they had essentially in common. Colonisation did not negate the fact that both the colonised and the coloniser were human, rational beings who possessed the capacity to communicate and generate common meaning, even if this capacity was unequally developed in different demographics.

"If intelligence is common to us all, then so is the reason that makes us rational beings; and if that be so, then so is the reason that prescribes what we should do or not do. If that be so, there is a common law also; if that be so, we are fellow citizens; and if that be so, the world is a kind of state. For in what other common constitution can we claim that the whole human race participates? And it is from there, from this constitution, that our intelligence and sense of law derive; or else, where could they come from?" (Marcus Aurelius.

Meditations. Translated by Robin Hard. Oxford University Press, 2011, 4:4)

With the growth of empires, universal humanity became an explicitly meaningful idea, a new possibility of universal belonging associated with higher degrees of conscious agency, and the price to pay was the same for everyone: to transcend their cultural conditioning and group identity and embrace what all humans have intrinsically in common. The new sense of belonging required either a leap of faith or a feat of transcendental reasoning, and many cultures were not ready for this structural transformation, trapped by the ritualised absoluteness of their mythical reality.

Being immersed from birth in the culture of heroic ancestors and serving as a ritualistic conduit to ancient 'mysteries' may feel like a profound spiritual connection, a source of personal grounding, moral authority and power, but it is also a developmental limit for the uniquely human capacity to generate meaning. The essence of culture is repetition, eternal recurrence. It is not an expression of reflexive consciousness and creative agency but something that happens to us, something we can either submit to, or transcend. When different cultures cohabitate on the same territory, their conflicting norms are irreconcilable within the traditional frameworks and can be managed either through violence, which is ultimately catastrophic to one of the parties, or through rational organisation, associated with greater consistency of reflexive relations. The latter possibility requires a fundamental change in social attitude, from moral conviction and narrative completeness to rational introspection and public justification. The distinguishing property of rational organisation vis-a-vis the assimilated cultural norms is the capacity to begin from incompatible states of conditioning, develop a common language, resolve cultural inconsistencies and generate common meaning. Our conversation begins where culture ends.

The generative principle that resulted in the civilisational achievements of architecture, science and technology was, invariably, not culture but rationality. Culture was instrumental for containing and managing human instincts and the archaic forms of irrationality, and imposing a social bond based on more inclusive, homogenised irrationality (national pride, militarism or ethno-religious supremacism) and thus motivate inter-group cooperation beyond the clan-centric values. This could be accomplished in countless ways, as evinced by the diversity and variability of cultures, whereas the laws of sense were always the same for all civilisations. Those who could channel the creative power of logic to social ends produced extraordinary things, timeless wonders, despite their traditions, not because of them.

Traditional cultures, no matter how civilised, are inherently repressive, enforcing contingent customs whose function is to sustain the illusion of moral authority as the organising principle of the community. By implication, culture has social utility commensurate with the degree to which the moral authority of the group is objectively deficient, and only then it must be repressed and artificially organised to prevent its disintegration. The utility of culture is exhausted over time by its inherent contradictions, which lead to nihilism and ultimately to systemic collapse. This consequence can be averted only by rational consciousness transcending culture, all culture. Once the objective moral norms are commonly discernible there is no need for the constraints of culture; the objective reality of being Human spontaneously takes the place of culture. Nevertheless, the sense of universal Humanity is not easy to accomplish.

The first major step on the path to moral universalism was the emergence of monotheistic religions. The essential feature of the transition from polytheism to monotheism was the rejection of normative plurality, associated with different domains of existence and the idiosyncratic conceptions of mystical power, vs. normative singularity across all possible domains and categories. Paul Tillich interprets the difference between polytheism and monotheism in *Theology of Culture* in terms of justice: "The unlimited claim of any god of space destroys the universalism implied in the idea of justice. This and this alone is the meaning of prophetic monotheism. God is one God because justice is one." Moreover, justice can be one only if truth is one, and truth can be one only if the structure of meaning is one, based on universal rules of sense, it is therefore no coincidence that One God became synonymous with Logos, signifying the conceptual trinity of supreme moral authority, language and sense. God is one because Truth is one, God is one because Logic is one, God is one because Reality is one, and crucially, if God is one then Humanity, 'made in the image of God', is also one, despite not being equally true to the 'image' (Logos) in which Humanity was made. The symbolic meaning of 'the original sin' consists in a voluntary or negligent alienation from Logos (the laws of sense) by means of a performative contradiction, thereby negating the moral authority and the creative power over meaning that is constitutive of human consciousness. By coveting and reaching out for 'the knowledge of good and evil' which is intrinsically within us, always already ours, and subject to which we are already held responsible as autonomous agents, we negate our moral authority and its ideal, the perfect image of consciousness in which human agency is made, and we thus become alienated within ourselves, fragmented: a dis-integrated Self. The primordial harmony of Logos consists in its perfect integrity, hence morality and agency are two sides of the same coin, normative and ontological (see Kowalik Michael. Transcendental Theology for Non-Believers. African Journal of Humanities and Social Sciences, 2022).

The monotheistic paradigm radically transcended the tribal mindset by building on the ancestor-authority that characterised tribalism and progressively extending the scope of this authority to all human beings, subject to the phenomenological criterion of 'human likeness' (*anthropos*). The established ethic of submission to a personified arch-father was universalised and combined with the idea of the ultimate self-interest of every human being, centred on avoiding negative spiritual consequences in the metaphysical hereafter. The transcendent Self was understood as eternal, therefore any advantage that applied only for the life of the body had to be measured against the eternal interest of the Self. In this moral calculus, the metaphysical interest could not be defeated by any temporary costs, providing the adherents of monotheistic religions with a powerful motive to obey the authoritative demands of the arch-father, mediated by the priesthood and coordinated by the symbolism of the Church. This paradigm dominated for Millennia, but as the Age of Enlightenment explicated the power of logic, the scripturally fixed religious dogma grew increasingly incompatible with the evolving awareness of the structure of meaning, relying on complex symbolic interpretations to retain its diminishing capacity to persuade. The language of spiritual consequences had to be updated to be meaningful in contemporary terms and consistent with the changing conception of 'the world as we know it'.

If there is no God then anything may be permitted, or if the real God does not command anything but 'shines like the Sun and everything grows because of it', then anything may also be permitted, and if anything is permitted then why should I not kill another if I can get away with it, or if it is legally sanctioned, or if it 'saves lives' and benefits the majority? In order to consistently answer these questions, moral consequences must be substantiated without appealing to God, or else the function of God must be explained and justified without appealing to religion, in logically consistent terms that necessitate moral consequences that affect everyone's self-interest.

Self-interest is logically indispensable to moral reasoning. It is tautologically true that intentional action must be motivated by self-interest or it would not be motivating to Self and we would not do it. By acting intentionally we satisfy Our preferences for acting in a particular way, irrespective of whether those preferences are beneficial to others or strictly selfish. Even when the intended action is perceived as distressing or harmful to Self, or performed under duress, we can only intend it (or intend to comply with coercion) if we judge it as preferable to any alternative course of action available to us. In every case of intending to act there is also the second-order preference for having the intention 'to act in a particular way' satisfied rather than not satisfied: in intending to $\varphi$ we affirm that it is preferable (or more valuable) to $\varphi$ than not to $\varphi$, where $\varphi$ stands for 'exercise the capacity <to act in a particular way>'. This second-order preference is centred on agency per se, on the value of exercising one's will that is constitutive of rational consciousness and is distinct from the value of specific actions.

It is not logically possible for an agent to intentionally act against and thus be negatively committed to one's own contemporaneous preference for acting intentionally, or to exercise the freedom to discriminate between more or less valuable actions without already unequivocally affirming the preference for being a conscious rational agent. The commitment to value rational agency is intrinsic to agency, presupposed by all contemporaneous value-commitments; it is the ultimate self-interest. "I must see myself as having unconditional value - as being an end in myself and the condition of the value of my chosen ends - in virtue of my capacity to bestow worth on my ends by rationally choosing them." (Markovits, Julia. Moral Reason. Oxford University Press, 2014, 103)

Given that self-interest underpins all intentional action, morality must be reducible to rational self-interest or it would not be rational to be moral, therefore wrong to be moral, therefore nonsense. Morality, insofar as it is a normative principle, must therefore comply with the laws of logic to allow consistent determinations of what is moral and who is right in cases of moral disagreement. The only relevant distinction that makes self-interested action either morally right or wrong is whether and to what extent we are rational about it. A possible objection to this argument is that humans may possess an intrinsic moral conscience that reflects the objective conditions of existence, the totality of being, independently of individual rationality. I contend that, a) the conditions of existence or the totality of being must also comply with the laws of logic in order to be true, otherwise they would be nonsensical and therefore meaningless, and b) even if moral conscience is intrinsically normative it is still necessary to consistently interpret what it requires and rationally justify that we ought to obey it. If moral conscience is the source of morality then it too must fully comply with the laws of logic to allow consistent determinations of what is right in cases of moral disagreement. The basis of morality must make sense, irrespective of how it is identified, or it would be nonsense.

In search of rational norms, the rule of law diverged from religion and sought to ground itself in the best interest of society as a whole, determined by a supremely educated professional order on the basis of rational deliberation and the persuasive authority of past legal judgments. The new system identified its basic norm in the contemporary factors of social utility for the greatest number, limited only by agreed upon universal rights and a handful of special prerogatives. The utilitarian paradigm was progressively adopted as the secular framework of moral judgement, providing the dominant institutions with a supposedly moral and objective justification for social censure and selective repression, but the underlying value-judgement still begged the question, presupposing the normative conclusion (of what is 'objectively' right or wrong, just or unjust) rather than proving it. Critically, the utilitarian norm is not grounded in universal self-interest and does not have the capacity to resolve cultural conflicts about values and therefore necessitates violence, which it must monopolise in order to maintain the logical continuity of its normative standard. Moreover, since social utility is prioritised over universal human rights during emergencies and wars, it is susceptible to regressing to the primitive model of dominance by force alone, under the guise of proportionality or greater good. I will comprehensively challenge the normative status of these concepts in Part 2.

The phrase 'the rule of law' is central to the doctrine of political authority. It implies not only that someone rules, but that someone rules 'because of' and 'according to' law, in order to fulfil the law. The authority to rule necessarily derives from the law; the law cannot derive from the authority to rule unless the authority is already lawful, which implies that the authority to rule derives from the law, therefore contradiction. The alleged authority of any national Constitution already begs the question, presupposing the existence of some unspecified law that the constitution aims to fulfil. What is the Law? The lawmakers are yet to justify themselves. The most consistent substitute for the intrinsically authoritative, universal law is that each is bound by whatever idea of law they seek to impose on others, that each is to be judged by their own standard of judgement, but this model of law is also normatively ungrounded.

The system of law engages with the liability for reasonably predictable and determinate consequences of individual actions, but since individual consciousness is not ontologically self-sufficient but socially mediated, where irrationality and moral errors affect reflexive consciousness, therefore all meaning and identity, a broad metaphysical effect is also incurred. This systemic effect is a consequence of the unconscious tendencies that evade the formal criteria of guilt and restorative justice and yet we are all indirectly disciplined by it, as it conditions the causal chain of events we experience as reality. Error begets error; unidentified moral wrongs and irrationality corrupt 'the world as we know it' and degrade the systemic capacity for moral discernment. Reality is a process of systemic justice where every action has universal consequences and therefore nothing can be hidden and no agent can escape the systemic, ontological liability. Whereas the legal concept of justice is in part conventional, culturally relative and objectively unjust insofar as it is normatively contingent, the effect of socially mediated moral wrongs on the shared conditions of existence is perfectly objective, real, logically necessary, therefore systemically 'just', even if this kind of justice does not identify the underlying moral wrongs or provide conclusive restitution for the most affected individuals. The restitution it offers is conditional on becoming aware of our own moral errors. It is an ideal we aim at when we think about justice but erroneously remove ourselves from the sphere of moral liability. The conditions of existence do not explicitly inform us what we ought to do but provide general moral feedback that appeals to rational self-interest by subjecting all agents to systemic, social consequences of individual choices.

Reality is an unconscious mechanism of justice that disciplines without assuming moral authority or the specificity of justice-oriented intentions. It amounts to determinism about consequences but does not determine whether the original intentions are morally right or wrong in virtue of their consequences. Moral discernment requires conscious authority, and conscious authority requires motivation.

Is an intrinsically authoritative moral framework, grounded in self-interest, possible? Since the world as we know it is limited to what makes sense, constituted as a logically consistent system of relations, we can infer that the fundamental laws of logic - the conditions of sense - are an intrinsic property of the world. If morality is an ontologically indispensable feature of social relations, which are a part of the world as we know it, then morality must be rational, universal and therefore true independently of contingent social conventions, therefore not a function of democratic representation, consensus, implied consent or a result of any other 'legitimisation process' but aligned with what is objectively right, implying moral realism. On this view, logical consistency demands that every rational being has the moral authority to do what is morally right and no authority, under any circumstances, to do what is morally wrong. We must also understand the rule of law as an attempt to formalise what is morally right vs. morally wrong, because the objective moral law is the only rational basis of legal authority insofar as it proscribes or prohibits. The idea of having the authority to do what is objectively wrong is absurd, contradictory in its premises. Without moral realism all institutional authority is false and everyone claiming to be a figure of authority is an impostor.

The basis of moral authority consists in the socially mediated capacity for rational thought, by means of which we are able to collectively generate meaning and bestow worth on our aims. By acting intentionally on reasons taken to be our reasons we affirm the value of rational agency, which is the ultimate self-interest. All contingent value-categories are conditional on the capacity for meaning, therefore on conscious rational agency. It follows from the axiom of subjectivity that we cannot devalue other beings of the same kind without reflexively devaluing both ourselves and our own values and, consequently, diminishing our capacity to consistently realise our intentions as rational agents. Our ultimate interest is conditional on valuing the same interest in others as much as we value it about ourselves, therefore the value of rational agency has absolute priority over tribal, racial, cultural or ideological identities. To ascribe moral priority to any subordinate category is to implicitly negate the basis of its value and thus contradict its priority. Similarly, all ideologies that devalue the rational agency of others on account of their otherness contradict themselves, implicitly negate their own value and authority. In order to be wholly oneself, to be a fully integrated being, to be fully human, absolutely valuable, of inviolable moral status, and to act with full moral authority, one must abandon all contradictory value commitments.

The distinction between right and wrong can be discerned by morally imperfect agents only indirectly, not by inquiring what is moral, which is inescapably tainted by our own cultural conditioning and moral errors, but by inquiring what kind of normative distinctions are rational and thus deduce the logical conditions of morality by *a priori* reasoning. It is possible to identify and refute any beliefs that are not logically consistent (imply contradiction) and refine the social norms on the basis of systemic consistency and objective grounding. Confusion and disagreements about values and norms compel us to deliberate towards a logically provable, universal moral standard, because hiding from one another behind culturally impervious borders is not a viable solution to moral disagreement.

Never in history were humans as united, as familiar and as understanding as we are today. The internet has brought us closer together than any leader, religion or ideology of the past. We are often told the opposite, but the alleged fragmentation of the world is superficial, driven by over-focalisation and political exploitation of disagreements about cultural norms and ideological commitments. Beneath these disagreements we are participating in unprecedented global discourse, testing the universal criteria of sense vs. nonsense, and thus cultivating the capacity to understand one another and resolve disagreements according to common, intuitively recognised rules. By communicating, even just by expressing our frustrations and reasons for disagreeing, we already generate meaning, common meaning, and we progressively integrate our rational capacities as one communication community. Rational discourse is of itself a transformative experience, a tide that raises all boats. We are witnessing the natural death of tribalism and religious supremacism and experience the emergence of a universal connection that was never experienced before, of meaning that was not received but consciously created by us. The more we try to understand the reasons for our disagreements the more powerful and conscious we become as a kind.

The ultimate test of individual moral authority is to reject every group-identity and stand alone with other humans. Only then we can become fully integrated, fully human. For some it will be like stepping off a cliff, for others it will be like flying. Humanity is one because rationality is one.

## Ontological conditions of moral status

Objective morality entails objective moral status, which consists in the fact that moral law applies only to status-holders, including the imperative to give moral consideration to all status-holders. The challenge of moral philosophy is not to presume the moral status of a particular kind of entity - this would violate the principle of sufficient reason and therefore the law of non-contradiction - but to prove that moral status is a true property of a particular entity for other entities. Retracing the philosophical attempts to prove the moral status of humans may reveal the magnitude of this challenge and the logical limitations of morality as a normative principle.

In the second part of the XVIII century Immanuel Kant examined the logical consequences of purpose-oriented reasoning, concluding that any person who unconditionally values their capacity for rational action, which is a priori true of every rational agent, is logically committed to act in a privileged way towards all rational beings (the Categorical Imperative).Another way, to value rational agency in myself entails valuing it as a matter of principle, in every human, unconditionally, and above all else. It is generally understood that "when Kant refers to our humanity, he has our rational capacities in mind. Our humanity, according to Kant, simply is our (distinctively human) capacity for self-directed rational behaviour" (Ibid. Markovits, 83). In the words of Kant (Groundwork of the Metaphysics of Morals. Cambridge University Press, 1998, 4:389): "when [moral philosophy] is applied to the human being it does not borrow the least thing from acquaintance with him (from anthropology) but gives to him, as a rational being, laws a priori..." This view of humanity was not entirely new but a refinement of Plato's definition of 'man' that did not emphasise self-ideation: "The name 'man' (ἄνθρωπος) indicates that other animals do not examine, or consider, or look up at any of the things that they see, but man (...) considers that which he has seen."(Plato. Cratylus, 399c) The basis of universal moral law is evidently not any empirical or cultural feature, not even the category of Homo sapiens, but rational, reflexive consciousness. Nevertheless, Kantian analysis does not establish a practical link between self-interest and moral conduct. Kant does not claim that, in all circumstances, compliance with the moral law would individually benefit us more and therefore should motivate us more than any strategic advantage derived from violating it. Why be moral if we can get away with immorality? Why apply the same moral standard to all if we can profit from applying it selectively or hierarchically? An additional difficulty in interpreting the concept of universal moral law arises due to the practical asymmetry in the individual expressions of the principle of rationality: humans are neither perfectly rational nor equally rational, not only as able adults but as infants and people with psychiatric disorders or disabilities, and it is unclear how and to what extent a superior individuation of the principle of rationality ought to rationally respect and value an inferior individuation of rationality apart from valuing rationality 'in principle', that is, as an ideal. Human irrationality, which in effect 'dehumanises' the entity acting irrationally or non-rationally, is *prima facie* beyond the scope of the moral law, creating a gap between the idealised Categorical Imperative and its rational application in real situations.

The next significant contribution to the scholarship of rational morality came from Christine Korsgaard. Building on the work of Kant, she developed a system of ethics combining the premise that rational agency is conditional on social-reflexivity (seeing others as beings of the same ontological kind) and the idea of 'integrity' of consciousness. "The function of the normative principles of the will", writes Korsgaard (The Sources of Normativity. Cambridge University Press, 1996, 229), "is to bring integrity and therefore unity – and therefore, really, existence – to the acting self." The relevant sense of the term 'integrity' combines both ethical and ontological aspects: the integrity of conduct and the integrity in the sense of a structurally unified, whole, cohesive and internally consistent individual being; an unequivocal Self: "To be a thing, one thing, a unity, an entity; to be anything at all: in the metaphysical sense, that is what it means to have integrity." Conversely, to lose integrity "is to no longer be able to think of yourself under the description under which you value yourself and find your life to be worth living and your actions to be worth undertaking." (Ibid. 102) When we lose moral integrity we also metaphysically dis-integrate, become fragmented and thus progressively lose our capacity for conscious rational action and the capacity to both convey and generate meaning. The relevant moral imperative is that if we value our existence as conscious rational agents then we are rationally committed, in self-interest, to act in such a way as to maximise the degree of our existence as conscious rational agents, which is commensurate with integrity.

The second step is Korsgaard's argument was to show that we identify as human beings (in the Kantian sense) only by regarding the humanity of others in the same way as our own humanity. Social-reflexivity and reciprocal recognition of personal value is then of ontological importance to all agents, creating a system of mutually dependent interests. This still essentially Kantian approach was possibly inadequate in several respects: 1) like Kant, Korsgaard did not advance a solution to the asymmetries in the expression of conscious rational agency (humanity) among humans with respect to the moral law; 2) it is unclear whether and why the property 'human' should be regarded as equally valuable in all individuals despite being unequally expressed, as implied by the differences in 'integrity' that correspond to degrees of consciousness that may, at the lower end of the spectrum, be akin to the unconscious forces of nature; 3) the causative link between moral action and the degree of existence as a conscious rational agent ('integrity') was not analytically demonstrated. This does not undermine Korsgaard's theory but calls for refinement of the argument from 'integrity' in practically meaningful terms. The three concerns identified above were already analysed in detail, but the last concern warrants additional remarks about the phenomenological context.

Earlier work in phenomenology has already demonstrated that the condition of social-reflexivity applies to every aspect of conscious identity. Thomas Nagel argued that for an organism to have "conscious experience at all means, basically, that there is something it is like to be that organism." (What is it Like to Be a Bat? The Philosophical Review, 1974, 436) More generally, the question of 'what it is like to be me' exemplifies a fundamental property of reflexive consciousness that cannot be meaningfully answered just in terms of the atomic *me*, as 'I am *me*' or 'I am like *me*', without falling prey to circular reasoning, or in terms of pure difference, the otherness from the other, the non-identity with the other, which is trivially true of everything and has no identifiable remainder. Unless I can co-identify with something else there is literally nothing *like* being me, no terms of identification, no content of identity, therefore no sense to the proposition that I am a definite something. Every meaningful aspect of my identity entails the awareness that in that particular respect I am in fact identical to someone or something else. Like a finger that cannot point at itself, conscious agency is not ontologically self-sufficient but constituted in terms of identity relations with other beings of the same kind. It follows that I can be myself only indirectly, socially, by consistently identifying with what I identify others as. If my intentions or attitude would negate any common property of other individuals who are like me, I would be undermining my ontological integrity as a conscious agent. Another way, whatever property I value about myself I am rationally committed to value about others and for others, or I stand to devalue it in myself and for myself, and consequently diminish my agential capacity to consistently realise intentions. We can thus derive moral status from the socially-reflexive ontology of rational agents.

Humanity is rational agency, which is a matter of degree, but it is phenomenologically mediated, conceived of in terms of human likeness, which is a necessary condition of mutual recognition as instances of reflexive consciousness, therefore a necessary condition of reflexive communication, therefore of meaning and self-ideation, therefore also a necessary condition of rational agency and personhood. The phenomenological image of humanity does not coincide with the quality of expression or the degree of rational agency at a particular time, or age, or under any contingent circumstances, but engages with the temporally continuous personal identity that includes expressions, capacities and potentialities manifested or anticipated in the lifetime of the person as a member of our ontological kind. The two conditions - rationality and likeness to kind - are ontologically co-dependent, meaningless without one another. We invoke both conditions by seeing ourselves *in* another, in a sleeping person, in an unconscious person, in a disabled person or an infant, already by recognising them as *another*. Are they expressing or possessing any essential characteristics that I value about myself, that make me a conscious rational agent? If the answer is *yes* then we reflexively affirm their moral status, and if we would unwittingly violate it then we diminish those characteristics in ourselves and for ourselves, hence diminish our humanity, our integrity, our agency, the degree of our consciousness, which can only be reflexively sustained, reflexively meaningful.

The moral status of an entity is true for a conscious agent only if the intrinsic value of the agent would be negated by his indifference to the intrinsic value of the entity, and the intrinsic value of the entity would be negated by its indifference to the intrinsic value of the agent. Moral status is socially reflexive; it is necessarily held in common by entities capable of moral reciprocity.

Rational ethics dictates that self-interest can be reliably served only by seeing oneself as a moral being among other beings of the same kind. The phenomenological sense of 'seeing oneself as another' is associated with the most basic moral feedback. Man is a mirror. Consciousness is a mirror. When you degrade the image of Man you reflexively degrade your own consciousness.

The phenomenological aspect of rational consciousness is prominently manifested in human experience. For example, all deformed representations of the human form evoke instinctive disgust, or horror, because we are a product of over one hundred thousand years of phenomenological conditioning in what humanity 'is like', which guides our aesthetic sensibility and ontological sensitivity. The human form, especially the face, constitutes the phenomenological foundation of our socially reflexive consciousness, our 'first language', therefore everything that de-faces or de-forms the innately programmed human identity also subverts our individual meaning and being; it is phenomenologically aberrant. We dress our dead in fine garments, we lay them out neatly in caskets, not just because it is culturally forced on us but in order not to witness the deformity and degradation of the human form accomplished by death. Similarly, anything identifiable as non-human but endowed with realistic human features, including machines, may be experienced as phenomenologically aberrant, anti-reflexive, a caricature of our kind. Our integrity as conscious individuals is phenomenologically mediated and it is not possible to fully disentangle who we are from the identity-grounding impressions of our kind. Certain professions and art critics can act as if they are perfectly comfortable with grotesque representations of the human form, but on a deeper personal level this produces an ontological split, a contradiction between the phenomenological conditions of our being and the conceptual object of aberrant fascination. No matter how skilfully and persistently we can contextualise and bracket-off the aberrant (as symbolic, progressive, transcendent, cultural, inclusive etc) we cannot remain unaffected on the structural level of self-integration.

The process of meaning-creation according to the laws of sense is essential to conscious agency, but it is also inseparable from the phenomenological dimension that grounds mutual recognition as instances of rational consciousness, without guaranteeing it. Any action that is inconsistent with these conditions disrupts the reflexive structure of the Self. On this view, humanity is a 'flat' property when considered phenomenologically, as mutual recognition, but Humanity is also a matter of degree when considered in the more essential sense of rational consciousness, as the degree of the ontological integrity of the Self. The former sense of human identity, the face, orientates us towards one another, allows for mutual recognition as conscious beings and already initiates the conversation, but does not of itself constitute value or entail moral status. The latter sense of Humanity is the highest value, the measure of all value, the basis of moral status and who we essentially are; it is the primary 'likeness' that matters to conscious agency when we recognise the face of another and communicate.

The value-commitment to rational agency is not arbitrary, but something we affirm in every action, by choosing to act in a particular way. All rational agents are always already engaged in the creation of meaning, and thus, by virtue of rational consciousness, belong to one communication community based on this essential value-commitment. Moral status, in the objective, realist sense, is reducible to the value of rational agency.

The integrity of rational consciousness does not depend on reflexive relating with animals or nature or ecosystems, since these categories are only products of rational consciousness, always an 'it' and not a reflexive Self. No logical inconsistency arises in our constitution when we do not recognise animals or ecosystems as our moral equals, or as possessing intrinsic moral worth that could be in conflict or on the same continuum with the moral worth of rational agency. These categories of being are not socially reflexive vis-a-vis Humanity and do not value rational agency, since they either do not possess it or do not reflexively express it, therefore valuing them on par with rational consciousness would be contrary to rational consciousness and self-interest. Moreover, 'nature' and 'ecosystems' are not social entities and cannot be plausibly regarded even as 'individual beings' of another kind but vague abstractions imposed on the multiplicity of the world as 'we' know it. In the context of objective ethics, environmental destruction is wrong not because ecosystems possess moral status in their own right but because the environment is an existentially significant common resource that has value to rational agents and we are morally responsible for actions that indirectly affect other rational agents.

The question of the moral status of animals is more nuanced. Many animal species are inherently social, some share meaningful phenomenological features with Homo sapiens, and some are selectively bred to be social, affectionate and protective of humans, which makes a range of animal species personable. Nevertheless, the absence of reflexive relating as rational agents precludes even the most personable animals from possessing an objective moral status as formalised in the present work, but does not preclude non-moral reasons to value and care for them. Cruelty to animals is wrong not because animals are endowed with objective moral features but because cruelty entails contradictory value-commitments. It amounts to personifying the object of cruelty and simultaneously degrading that personified object, therefore reflexively degrading oneself. Cruelty itself is immoral, therefore inhuman.

## Logical consistency determines the integrity of conscious agency

The structure of meaning, entailed by the laws of sense, is all-encompassing. The relation of self-identity 'A is A' is possible only in relation to not-A, the background and context that delimits every attribute of A, therefore 'everything else' is differentially implicated in the identity of A. This is the negative condition of identification that incorporates the whole world. The positive condition of identifying A as a particular instance of something is the category of A's, differentiated from other categories, which permits A's attribution to that category and answers the question 'what is A?' in terms of what it is like but not identical to. The ability to identify a tree, for example, presupposes an idea of what trees are like. 'A is A' also means that nothing else can be identical to this A, or it would be just this A, therefore not something else. This is the sense of the law of identity and, by implication, of the law of non-contradiction and the law of excluded middle, which together comprise the structure of sense.

The three fundamental laws of logic are not a contingent set of axioms but the necessary conditions of sense, the limits of meaningful thought, therefore the necessary conditions and limits of the world as we know it, therefore the three laws are also laws of nature. Without the fundamental laws there is only non-sense, no-identity, no-thing, hence those who earnestly deny the fundamental laws are also earnestly nihilistic about individuality, reality, perception and being. Nevertheless, the structure of sense is normatively minimal; it does not tell us what any integrated object of thought ought to be but only what it cannot be. To violate the laws of sense is to convey no integrated idea. Sense is therefore fundamental to reflexive consciousness, to the idea of being, to perception of being, and to the possibility of mutual understanding. We are relying on it now: I, to express the intended meaning and you to understand and reflect on it. We could not exist for one another without it.

Every violation of the laws of sense is non-sense, a hole in consciousness, empty of meaning, which implies that irrationality/illogicality is not a state of the Self but, to appropriate a Lacanian term, a state of *absense*, a pocket of unconsciousness within the logical space of meaning and subjectivity. The absense undermines the wholeness/integrity of the Self, subverting our intentions, distorting our aims, corrupting our speech. Every aspect of subjective consciousness we abandon to absense becomes a province that is vulnerable to possession by another or by the deterministic, unconscious forces of nature, which are in motion but engender nothing new, akin to eternal recurrence. The first stage of incremental dis-integration towards unconsciousness may be the loss of a temporally continuous, consistent identity, replaced by multiple, context-dependent personas with incompatible moral characteristics. Dis-integration consists in cultivating a self-image that is logically inconsistent, therefore not consistently reflexive: it cannot be grasped as One. In particular, an irreflexive attitude assumed in relation to other beings of the same kind reflects in the dissolution of reflexive consciousness in oneself.

Based on the logical model of reflexive consciousness, the loss of integrity causes the incremental loss of subjective capacities; the inability to identify, resist or change the established behavioural patterns. He who cannot not be a tyrant, who cannot not be a murderer, who cannot not be a liar, who cannot stop the habit of violence, deception or greed, is not a conscious Self in that context, not there even to oneself, but a blind force of nature playing itself out as violence, deception or greed. This deterministic state is brought about by incremental, implicit renunciation of the Self, renunciation of conscious rational agency.

Since reflexive consciousness is socially mediated, strong affinity with a group characterised by context-dependent moral inconsistencies may be the most common path to individual self-disintegration. Terrible things done by groups of individuals against those who are dehumanised on the basis of a designated type or identity are an expression of the most primal forces, mediated by culture, which is still only a temporally constrained force of nature. Forces of nature are perpetually in conflict with one another, fixated on one another, absorbed by one another, and mutually exhaust one another. This primordial conflict can be transcended by rational consciousness but, at times, no resistance to mass aberration is possible; one can only step out of the way. Let the violent ones deal with the violent ones, according to their unconscious tendencies, and those who know better may step aside and let the deterministic forces of nature keep one another in check. Those who fail to resolve existential disagreements by rational deliberation are compelled to fight to the death, and ultimately erase one another.

In every political conflict both sides make a critical moral choice long before the conflict becomes kinetic, before mutual killing begins. Every totalitarian dystopia is unwittingly brought about by the moral deficiencies of the majority, by a series of cumulative moral errors that are socially accepted, which in turn increase the likelihood of further moral errors, towards a systemic collapse of moral conscience. Beyond that point the system becomes wholly deterministic, driven purely by animal forces, and only total exhaustion of energy and resources can return the agitated demographics to a non-deterministic, partially conscious, reflexive state.

An individual who is committed to the laws of sense, relatively immune to the prevailing ideologies and political affectations, cannot regard the deterministic majority as equally consistent and true to the human-kind. Humanity, being a synthesis of conscious rational agency and phenomenological affinity, is a matter of degree. The largely invariant baseline of phenomenological likeness-to-kind typically dominates in a stable society, but it too can be degraded by the dehumanising inconsistencies of those who 'merely look alike'. The compulsive projection of resentment or conviction seeks to mirror itself, to unconsciously repeat itself without rational invalidation, and if the sentiment is not reciprocally affirmed then one is instantly dehumanised and excluded. This mode of unconscious interaction consists in the passive re-enactment of conditioning without any creation of common meaning. The persistent signalling by others that You do not belong in their circle of validation genuinely alienates, but also polarises conscious agency on the ontological level. We evolve as different, incompatible kinds, and only one kind can prevail.

It is not enough to merely survive alienation, but to endure it without mirroring and thus psychologically internalising the aberrant in the negative sense of 'opposition' or 'resistance'. In order to maintain integrity one must step aside of the deterministic, social moment, and this requires a lot of sense and a little luck. One must disassociate from the animal forces mediated by others without losing the reflexive connection to rational consciousness, including the phenomenological affinity for the subtlety of conscious presence. One must see deeper than the idealised human form, discern the likeness of those who are intentionally present, who consciously see into you and invite you to see into them, from those who are unconsciously carried by the forces of nature, going with the flow towards the great fall.

The kind of power that subjugates through violence does not matter to consciousness, like an earthquake does not matter to consciousness. When nature hurts us, we do not accuse nature of wrongdoing, we do not feel resentful. When a plague strikes, we burry our dead, we mourn, and we move on. When humans harm other humans, we see the perpetrators of the crimes committed against us as beings of the same kind, like us, but despicable. Unless we consciously resist this judgement, regard both violence and resentment as a force of nature rather than an act of rational consciousness, we grow resentful of our kind, and thus indirectly resent ourselves, and we ourselves become possessed by forces of nature. Resentment is essentially self-directed, metaphysical self-degradation; it can last for generations, it does not go away of its own accord but must be consciously resolved. The key to its resolution lies in our identification with humanity on the basis of rational consciousness rather than deterministic behaviour, but also requires discernment of that which unites us, makes us human: our capacity to collectively generate meaning.

When faced with a dis-integrated Self, it is not imperative to convince it that it is conflicted and false; it is its own challenge to transcend falsity, to become integrated, to choose integrity. Reality consists of the truth, it harbours no falsity, and everything that stands for falsity is bound to perish. If moral realism - the idea that moral wrongs have inescapable ontological consequences for the wrongdoer - is true, and it must be true for normative value judgements to make sense, to be grounded in reality, to be true, then it is also not imperative to resist the moral wrongs perpetrated by others but, insofar as they can be tolerated and endured, allow the fulfilment of moral consequences as a systemic, impersonal mode of justice and universal moral education.

The primary moral challenge in times of a widespread moral collapse is not to become what one hates, not to degrade oneself by anthropomorphising the inhuman, not to diminish rational consciousness, not to become a force of nature. This is how humanity is preserved even in times of horror. Humanity is never the enemy of a human; it is only the inhuman that can be the enemy of a human. The task of objective morality is to reliably discern the human from the inhuman within ourselves.

The integrity of conscious agency is conditional on the logical consistency of its self-conception with respect to the world as we know it, including other beings of the same kind. Everyone is convinced of the rationality of their choices at the time of choosing; otherwise we would not make those choices. Few reflect on the fact that by making a choice we set ourselves up to suffer the consequences of that choice if it happens to be irrational. When the attitude of conviction clashes with unexpected consequences, with suffering and failure, the laws of sense assert themselves without words. Our practical failures are self-evident when acting on outcome-oriented intentions, leaving behind a trace of temporal evidence on the basis of which we can diagnose our logical errors, whereas moral actions involve not only practical intentions but affect the integrity of our conscious agency and the associated freedom 'to choose otherwise'. This second-order effect interferes with our capacity to correctly identify moral consequences as detrimental to Self, as a case of failure; if the consequence of a moral wrong committed in the past is the present incapacity to choose otherwise, and we are not aware that we could choose otherwise if we acted morally right in the past, then we cannot discern from the present circumstances that being morally wrong has consequences. Moral action is the process via which we constitute ourselves as conscious agents, as creators of meaning, and the diminished state of our consciousness can morally inform us only when reflexively mediated by other conscious agents.

Moral judgement must be thought of as outcome-oriented to be motivating, and we can map this orientation with the formula of logical consistency. Everyone is convinced of the rightness of their moral choices at the time of choosing; otherwise they would not make those moral choices. Few reflect on the fact that by making a moral choice we set ourselves up to suffer the consequences of that choice if it happens to be wrong. When the attitude of moral conviction clashes with unexpected consequences for our conscious agency, for the integrity of the Self and for our capacity to choose otherwise, the authority of the moral law asserts itself without words.

Objective morality is necessarily logically consistent with the world as we know it, otherwise it would be non-sense. Mapping the logical consistency of self-in-the-world onto moral integrity is therefore essential to consistent moral discernment. This is the sense in which objective morality is aligned with the structure of meaning; morality is a sub-domain of sense. Irrational thought, which is to say non-sense, is the limit of self-integration and of the freedom to discriminate between right or wrong actions. It manifests as compulsive repetition and deterministic reaction, which is creative impotence. The degree to which we act in accordance with the fundamental laws of sense in the social dimension is the degree of our moral integrity, which is in turn coextensive with the capacity for freedom and the creative power over meaning. By generating common meaning/sense to resolve disagreements about norms, facts and values we collectively augment the conditions of existence, the content of the world as we know it.

Conscious agency is not free. It can be cultivated or it can be degraded and forfeited. Insofar as it is cultivated, it manifests as effortless ethical conduct, as creative originality and stability without resistance, because its power is imbued with the immutable authority of the truth, with the integrity of self-in-the-world that nothing can split apart and turn against itself. Everything contrary to it is absense. Insofar as conscious agency is forfeited, it manifests as the unconscious struggle between incongruent parts, each consumed by another's absense.

# Part Two: Practical Ethics

Practical ethics is concerned with the application of moral principles to specific problems, claims of right or types of action. In this section I consider how the general concepts identified in the formulation of the logical structure of consciousness apply to the criteria of mutual recognition, individual attitude, cultural narratives, values and normative practices.

## Prove your humanity

What does it mean to be human, what makes you human? Being human is evidently not just the human-like appearance, which presupposes what is yet to be proven. Your DNA and the electrical activity of the brain do not reveal the reflexive, rational consciousness that makes you an intentional, purposeful agent, a creator of meaning and a bestower of value. If there are no definitive empirical markers of rational consciousness then the only means of proving your humanity to another human - that you are a Self rather than 'it' - is via reciprocal communication, demonstrating that you are capable of purposefully generating common meaning. Since machines are capable of faking human faces, reasoning and emotive expression, our humanity is on notice; we must be better at expressing rational consciousness than the unconscious machines are at faking it, in order to prove that we are better, that our special moral status is justified.

Moral authority is conditional on being able to prove our humanity and, likewise, every established position of authority incurs this primary burden of proof. The challenge of proving one's humanity via creative communication is inherently reciprocal: in attempting to prove it we also test and evaluate the humanity of our interlocutor. One need not expect a conclusive test, but at least the kind of informal test that rational agents always used to discern moral standing: the test of consistency and reliability, identifying with those who are consistent and reliable in their will to understand others, generate common meaning to resolve disagreements, and distancing themselves from those who are not, who capitalise on disagreements rather than resolve them.

Can we possibly discern anything more? The following answer, which for the last seventy years was searching for the right question and hopefully found it here, comes from an unlikely source:

"Beyond the environment, man divines the presence of a 'something other' in both himself and others, which by virtue of its physiognomically impressive powers evokes the desire to know and is anxiously pondered. Thus the notion of the soul arises, as an image of everything in man which can never be causally known, as a counterworld to nature, as a mode of visualizing what will always be inaccessible by the light-world or the eye." (Henry Kissinger. The Meaning of History, 1950, 63) Human essence, despite being inaccessible to the senses, can be confirmed by the testimony of non-deterministic action: "Freedom [..] testifies to an act of self-transcendence which overcomes the inexorability of events by infusing them with its spirituality. The ultimate meaning of history - as of life - we can find only within ourselves." (Ibid. 23)

This is an astonishing insight, that the only proof of our humanity is our soul, and the soul entails the capacity for freedom, a dimension of meaning that machines cannot know, for the do not 'will'. The notions of Man and Machine are radically polarised by the inherently reflexive 'will to freedom': machines are inherently deterministic, even if we cannot fully describe the process of their determinations, whereas consciousness is intrinsically not. Looking back at human history, recognising the self-destructive madness of human behaviour, a question must now be asked that would be unacceptable at the beginning of this exploration: are there among us any counterfeit 'humans' who are deterministic, mere biological machines with a human face but without a soul. Are they the majority? An even more troubling question is whether this counterfeit humanity is present in us all, as a negative potential that can be realised as systematic unfreedom by a series of bad moral choices? Are we all counterfeit to various degrees?

Kissinger makes a final distinction between two aspects of reality, that of deterministic 'effect' and of non-deterministic 'experience': "As an effect it is subject to causal determination; as an experience it contains the meaning of freedom and the essence of personality" (Ibid. 116). I suggest there is more to this picture. Since the world exists for us only on account of our capacity to conceive of it, to make it meaningful and communicable, which is a result of the cumulative experience and creative thought of countless generations, then the deterministic world is also an expression of freedom, of the metaphysical freedom to think it subjectively, communicate it, and from these subjective moments engender a common, objective reality. Ironically, the deterministic machines and the counterfeit 'humans' can exist only in a world made of human freedom: the only world possible.

What then are the essential characteristics of free agency, capable of non-deterministic choice? All groups, insofar as they are identifiable by an ideology, are inherently deterministic, expressing a collectivised pseudo-agency where the belonging individual is not free to the extent of his belonging. It does not matter whether the group is a nation, a human rights advocacy network, or an anarchist collective - they are tools of determinism, not of freedom - but whereas a potentially free human has the capacity to willingly leave the group, a counterfeit cannot exist apart from the group; there is nothing else to 'it'. A free agent is always separate from the 'cause', never 'belongs' to any movement and does not communicate with groups but only with individuals, because only from this isolated position genuine human contact and the creation of common meaning are possible. Moreover without maintaining distance from the collectivised ideals, motifs and expectations of the group, without the will to think in one's own words, which is the essence of freedom, no moral conscience is possible. Freedom and therefore morality begin with voluntary exclusion, which is a matter of degree, of moral progress from natural determinism to Humanity.

How to become more human:

- accept that you do not belong anywhere,
- assume that there are no likeminded people (you just have not realised your disagreements yet),
- acknowledge that you have no tribe,
- accept that you are probably wrong about most things,
- but you need others to make sense of it all.

These are the likely prerequisites for higher degrees of self-integration but also for developing more sophisticated and less socially restrictive social systems. There is no ideal system that can be proposed to manage and solve the deficiencies of the individuals who comprise the system. The systems we have can only be as good as we ourselves are, and the path to becoming more conscious beings is rational discourse, which is of itself a transformative experience, a tide that raises all boats.

## Discourse ethics

I argued that maximising the degree of our existence as conscious agents is the ultimate self-interest, which is commensurate with the integrity of reflexive consciousness and is fulfilled by ethical conduct. It follows that ethical judgment may be validated by the consequent changes in the agent's metaphysical constitution. The axiom of subjectivity (Ibid. Kowalik 2020) implies that any change in the degree of conscious rational agency cannot be discerned directly by the agent whose degree of consciousness has changed, but only via reflexive relating with other individuals of the same degree of consciousness. The degree of consciousness is equal to the degree of logical consistency of reflexive relating with other beings of the same kind (likeness to kind), in terms of properties with respect to which all individuals of that degree are identical.

To sustain a particular degree of conscious agency requires the capacity for reflexive relating with other agents of that degree, which is conditional on having ontologically integrated the level of consistency characteristic of that degree. If an agent were to sincerely mirror the inconsistencies characteristic of a lower degree of rational consciousness, that agent would regress (dis-integrate) to the lower degree. It is not logically possible to be reflexively consistent with inconsistency. 'You shall not mirror the irrationality of others, lest you too would become irrational. You shall not engage with the aberrant in others as if it were an argument that warrants refuting; aberration becomes emptiness when faced with silence.'

The degree of conscious agency and the ontological integrity of Self depends not only on the relational consistency of the meaning-content of communication but also on the consistency of the attitude in communicating with the logical presuppositions of the act of communication. The latter type of reflexive consistency is typically referred to as 'discourse ethics'. Language is something we have in common, something we create by cooperating, and has meaning only because it is a medium of understanding 'between' us. According to Karl-Otto Apel "humanity is in essence linguistic, and therefore depends always already for its thinking on consensual communication." (Selected Essays: Ethics and the Theory of Rationality. Humanities Press International, 1996, 211) By verbalising our thoughts we are implicitly recognising another as a being capable of meaningfully responding to our arguments and we are inviting them to do so. "The logical justification for our thought" therefore commits us to "understand arguments critically" and to "mutually recognise each other as participants with equal rights in the discussion." (Ibid. 29) The consensual use of language presupposes a commitment to the common meanings of linguistic symbols and to the a priori criteria of sense, but it is also a gesture of facing one another as beings of the same kind; a reflexive symmetry of multiple instances of conscious agency in the same world. By engaging in communicative speech we enunciate our intention to cooperate in the use of language in order to accomplish mutual understanding, subject to the common rules of sense. The resulting understanding is not merely revelatory, not just a realisation of a meaning that is already there, but an original instance of sense; a narrative extension of the identity of being. Under these conditions, a non-cooperative use of langue and a non-reflexive attitude in communicating are both irrational: 'performative contradiction'.

The common function of propositional speech is to submit an incomplete construction of meaning/sense, an opinion, to the scrutiny of others in order to integrate it at a higher conceptual level by means of reciprocal argumentative responses. While some propositions may in fact be true, they are not 'known' to be true at the time of having an opinion; the sense of 'opinion' is to propose an explanation or justification as something unproven and therefore of unknown validity. Opinions can be interesting hypotheses, but hypotheses also presuppose not knowing whether the hypothesis is true or even adequately representative of a possible truth. The function of propositional speech is therefore not to tell the truth but, rather, to define an explanatory framework and set the terms of discourse. It involves implicit value judgements and subjective conceptual selections about the meaning of the problem itself; the question is either redefined or reinforced by the form of the answer.

It is contrary to the sense of speech to regard the incomplete meaning of an opinion as true by virtue of consensus, conviction or the desire to persuade others. It is also contrary to the sense of speech to deceive others, but not obviously so. A strategically motivated individual or group may ask: why should I be logically consistent about the presuppositions of discourse if my alleged irrationality helps me get what I want? The question thus posed is already logically defective, insofar as being logically inconsistent is precisely what limits our capacity to get what we want out of action: actions that are motivated by inconsistent beliefs work against one another and are ultimately self-defeating. Discourse ethics dictates that if our convictions motivate us to violate the presuppositions of discourse in order to influence and control others, then our capacity to think rationally and therefore to act effectively is also diminished, which in turn subverts the aim of benefiting from violating the presuppositions of discourse.

When two parties disagree with one another on a point of existential necessity they have only two choices: a) to reason from commonly recognised principles in order to resolve the disagreement, or b) to threaten the other party with violence if they do not submit. Beings who do not share the same laws of reason are limited to option (b). Historically, individuals who sought to avoid (b) in favour of (a) understood that any being that is capable of (a) is *anthropos* (one who is alike), and any being who is not demonstrably capable of (a) is ontologically deficient and morally inferior. Moreover, the capacity for (a) was recognised as commensurate with the capacity to understand and to be understood by others. Consequently, an individual who would demonstrate the capacity for communication, for example, by making meaningful demands, would implicitly affirm their capacity for reasoning on the basis of a common standard of reason. If the individual would then deny or contradict the common standard of reason, and thus pursue (b), their behaviour would be irrational and their speech rendered meaningless.

Language may be used asymmetrically and non-consensually without committing a performative contradiction, for example, when issuing voice commands to a machine. It is then not intended to accomplish mutual understanding but only as a physical prompt to facilitate a deterministic reaction. The meaning of language is inconsequential to the programmed reaction, which is conditional only on the transmission of sounds. Speech used in this way has no metaphysical dimension. The metaphysical dimension of language cannot be suppressed when consensually communicating with another conscious rational being; it is always reflexively invoked by speech in the consciousness of the listener and does not entail a determinist response. Conversely, if the interlocutor is intentionally irrational, denying the laws of sense presupposed in the use of language, or subverting the possibility of mutual understanding by non-cooperative, non-generative attitude in the use of speech, then silence is the only rational response, not the continuation of speech.

## Golden Rule

The reflexive symmetry of Self-in-Self and Self-in-Other was an integral part of moral philosophy for Millennia, in the form of the Golden Rule: "do to others what you would have them do to you". The rule was articulated in a number of ways: "In everything, do to others what you would have them do to you..." Matthew 7:12; "Treat others as you treat yourself..." Mahābhārata Shānti Parva 167:9; "Love your neighbour as yourself..." Leviticus 19:18. Despite being widely regarded as self-evident, the rule attracted scholarly criticism for failing to provide practical guidance for resolving moral disagreements and for being allegedly open to irrational outcomes. This criticism arose at least in part due to the failure to recognise the socio-ontological implications of moral logic.

Immanuel Kant, the most prominent critic of the Golden Rule, has proposed an alternative principle, known as the Categorical Imperative, aiming to overcome its perceived deficiencies: "Act only according to that maxim whereby you can, at the same time, will that it should become a universal law." (Groundwork of the Metaphysics of Morals. Cambridge University Press, 1998, 4:421). S. B. Thomas (Jesus and Kant. Mind, 1970, 199) nevertheless argues that "the Categorical Imperative and the Golden Rule are two sides of the same coin, so to speak, the former providing a clarification of the rational scope of the latter, and the latter providing the spiritual basis for the correct application of the former." I agree with this conclusion, albeit in regard to a different interpretation of the Golden Rule. I argue that the alleged metaethical limitations of the rule are not a deficiency but just what makes it effective as an intuitively intelligible, transformative attitude geared to socio-ontological grounding: it cultivates social-reflexivity as a constitutive feature of rational agency.

The Categorical Imperative was evidently not an attempt to re-interpret the Golden Rule but to transition from this circumstantial view of morality, conditional on personal inclinations, feelings or self-interest, to Metaphysics of Morality grounded in the "unconditional good" (Kant 4:399-401, 4:414). Kant reasoned that the Golden Rule fails in its alleged purpose because a consistent moral formula cannot be subject to contingent personal inclinations but, rather, our inclinations must be subordinated to universal moral norms. Vis-a-vis the Golden Rule, the principle of universality implies that consistent moral evaluation cannot be just about my interest vs. the interests of people I happen to be directly interacting with but about the interests of all people simultaneously. This is a crucial consideration since no action happens in social vacuum and what we do (or fail to do) with respect to one person may have profound secondary consequences for others (Reinikainen, J. The Golden Rule and the Requirement of Universalizability. Journal of Value Inquiry, 2005). How should I relate to a unique state of another if their constitution is different from mine? I cannot imagine what it would be like to be someone else insofar as we are constituted differently but only insofar as we are the same, perhaps only insofar as we are conscious rational agents indifferent circumstances. I may still be unable to relate to the relevant circumstances because I cannot-not experience them in the same way as someone who is constitutively different. What does the Golden Rule or the Categorical Imperative amount to in the face of such asymmetries?

Kant attempted to solve the problem of circumstantial asymmetries for the operation of the universal law by subordinating the moral criteria of action to what all rational agents have in common: "Act in such a way that you treat humanity, whether in your own person or in the person of any other, never merely as a means to an end, but always at the same time as an end." (Kant, 4:429) The central idea behind this move was to ground morality in what all rational agents value about themselves - the uniquely human capacity to bestow worth according to our will - which is indeed a property we have in common: "the value of humanity itself is implicit in every human choice" (Korsgaard 1996, 3.4.8). Humanity for Kant (4:389) means just conscious rational agency: his moral formula therefore implies that we are rationally committed not to infringe on the rational agency of others.

Notwithstanding the fact that all humans share the property of being conscious rational agents, which is socially expressed to various degrees, we may also be in radical disagreement about facts and values, and this kind of difference arguably impedes the consistent application of any moral or metaethical principle, including the Categorical Imperative. I can rationally treat others 'as myself' or with the same consideration as I have for myself only insofar as we are the same in the most relevant respect. That which is different can be made common only in terms of properties that are held in common, which for rational agents is rational consciousness, subject to the fundamental laws of sense. Rational agents aim at rationality in order to consistently realise their intentions, but are not consistently rational, therefore not consistently human, sometimes inhuman, and thus not reliably 'the same' in regard to the essential moral property underpinning the Categorical Imperative. The Kantian formula, despite sophisticated *a priori* grounding, presents us with a socially insurmountable practical challenge: every moral disagreement must be consistently worked out by inconsistent agents in unique circumstances.

Whereas the Kantian formula is too intellectually demanding to consistently negotiate in practice, the Golden Rule seems to fall short of the Categorical Imperative with respect to grounding: a mere assertion that something like the Golden Rule is universally imperative does not of itself constitute an authoritative argument in favour of the rule. It may be further objected that a rule which is not grounded in objective facts or an a priori argument is not a rule at all but a normatively empty assertion. Without such grounding, interpretations of the Golden Rule may vary widely and even reach contradictory conclusions. Historical variants of the rule do not explicitly identify who counts as 'your neighbour' or as 'others', potentially allowing for unlimited exclusions that are often found within the same textual sources (Leviticus 20:9-13; Deuteronomy 13:6-11). The rule is also deemed compatible with (or even reducible to) 'an eye for an eye' (Leviticus 24:19-20). A further theoretic step is therefore required to show that the alleged rule has objective normative force, that is, for a particular range of conditions there must be consistent, universally applicable reasons that count in favour of adherence to the rule that defeat any reasons to reject it.

Modern philosophers ascribed many implicit features to the Golden Rule that may be untrue. Specifically, the rule does not account for the uniqueness of circumstances or the differences between persons, it does not appeal to sympathy, universality, equality, the greater good, or the interests of others. On a literal reading, the rule seems to refer only to actions that would be desirable irrespective of situation, asking us to implicitly commit to absolute values. For example, if I do not want to be killed then I ought not to kill, ever, under any circumstances. Alternatively, if I want my life preserved by others then I ought to preserve the lives of others. The rule does not tell us what specific actions are wrong or what we ought to desire, but moral limits could emerge from its application heuristically, as a cumulative effect of our subjective wants and actions being confronted with the subjective wants and actions of others under various circumstances. The quality of what we want could thus progressively shape what we ought to want: a shared moral intuition geared to self-interest among beings of the same ontological kind. Without presupposing the ontological symmetry of person-to-person relations the notion of common morality would be nonsensical. The Golden Rule therefore expresses the relational grounding of moral content.

According to S. B. Thomas, who examined the Golden Rule in the context of Christian theology, "the awareness of himself as a Man-Type, rather than a man-particular, must have no doubt dominated Jesus' view of himself, and it may be pointed to as precisely that aspect of his self-awareness which makes him an instantiation of the Kantian imperative." (Ibid. Thomas 1970, 195-6) A perfectly rational application of the Categorical Imperative is, on this view, just how an ideal agent would apply the Golden Rule: as the ontological essence of Man-kind. "That which is prohibited by the Categorical Imperative, at the level of rational morality, is prohibited by Jesus' very being, at the existential or religious level. Anyone who partakes of his being, by finding in his projected in-dwelling in Him the sense of his own identity as Universal Man, will share this existentialized Categorical consciousness with Him also." (Thomas 1970, 196) S. B. Thomas does not attempt to develop the socio-ontological interpretation of the Golden Rule beyond the religious context, but it can be formally substantiated as an intrinsic property of rational agency, which in turn determines the degree of existence of man-particular with respect to Man-kind.

Thomas Nagel argued that "to recognize others fully as persons requires a conception of oneself as identical with a particular, impersonally specifiable inhabitant of the world, among others of a similar nature." (The Possibility of Altruism. Clarendon Press, 1970, 100) As discussed earlier, this applies also in reverse, which amounts to the logical equivalence between social reflexivity and conscious, individual existence: for an organism to have "conscious experience at all means, basically, that there is something it is like to be that organism." (Nagel 1974, 436) More generally, the question of 'what it is like to be me' exemplifies a fundamental property of reflexive consciousness that cannot be meaningfully answered just in terms of the atomic *me*, as 'I am *me*' or 'I am like *me*', without falling prey to circular reasoning. Unless I can co-identify with something else there is literally nothing *like* being me, therefore nothing like being anything *for* me, no terms of identification, no content of identity, therefore no sense to the proposition that I am a definite something. Like a finger that cannot point at itself, human agency is not ontologically self-sufficient but constituted in terms of identity relations with other beings of the same kind. It follows that I can be myself only indirectly, socially, by consistently identifying with what I identify others as, insofar as others identify reciprocally (social reflexivity). Another way, "the individual self will only emerge through the course of social externalization, and can only be stabilized within the network of undamaged relations of mutual recognition." (Habermas, Jürgen. The Future of Human Nature. Polity Press, 2003, 34)

In light of the above insight we can recast Nagel's formula as an explicitly ontological principle: to exist as a person requires a conception of oneself as identical with a particular, impersonally specifiable inhabitant of the world, among others of the same nature. Nagel has thus implicitly demonstrated that social reflexivity and everything it implies for rational agents is not a contingent moral convention but the ontological basis of conscious identity and therefore of agency. On this interpretation, the Golden Rule is not just a cultural or religious artefact but an expression of a universal law: social reflexivity grounds individual consciousness and is therefore objectively binding, insofar as we value our own existence as conscious rational agents. Moreover, if the degree of existence as a conscious rational agent is conditional on the consistency of reflexive relations with others, then the rule is also a means of transformation towards ideal agency, or, in the negative, a pathway of devolution from Man-kind towards unconscious, deterministic animal existence.

The Golden Rule does not of itself resolve moral disagreements but posits a metanormative framework of action based on the premise that our primary interest depend in a fundamental way on respecting the same interest in others. It does not prescribe how to be rational about ethics in particular circumstances but only radically limits the capacity to be irrational about our intentions, which may in turn guide social evolution towards ideal agency. Crucially, it does not entail a value-vacuum. Irrespective of our subjective preferences, the rule entails a practical commitment to social reflexivity, to the consistency of conduct, to the laws of sense, and, indirectly, to rational agency. The value of rational agency is implicitly affirmed in every action; it is the source of every contingent value commitment. This universal source of value is conditional on social reflexivity, which is therefore the objective normative standard for all agents. In addition to the socio-ontological considerations already discussed, the basic formulation of the rule expresses a profound psychological insight in inviting us to consider how we want to be treated by others before we act. The moment of reflexive contemplation that the rule is asking us to commit to has the capacity to mitigate impulsive, emotionally-driven reactions, but it is also transformative; a bonding experience able to progressively harmonise social relations. "The practice of the Golden Rule may be advocated precisely as a heuristic device to help the agent to become aware of the kinship of humankind." (Wattles, Jeffrey. The Golden Rule. Oxford University Press, 1996, 180) By reflecting on the Golden Rule we become aware of how our actions and attitudes can lead to responses that generate value. Based on this information we may adjust our standard of behaviour in order to reliably satisfy our intrinsic value-commitments, by respecting the same value-commitments in others. It is a transformative tool for rationally imperfect beings to reconcile the common need for cooperation with their competing claims on limited resources.

There is one recent objection to the validity of the Golden Rule that warrants a response. "The rule, it has been charged, cultivates blindness to the otherness of the other, since it assumes a basic commonality between agent and recipient. Some challenge the notion of a common humanity, citing the pervasive influence of differences such as gender, race, and class, and the uniqueness of individual personality." (Ibid. Wattles 1996, 174) I retort that without the presumption of common humanity (as conscious rational agency) we would not be of the human-kind, we would not exist as conscious rational agents and there would be no possibility of mutual understanding. Our ontological commonality underpins the capacity for individual uniqueness, which is therefore subordinate to this higher normative principle. In essence, our likeness-to-kind does not negate individual uniqueness but, rather, makes it meaningful and communicable. In adhering to the Golden Rule we learn how to integrate our consciousness vis-a-vis the consciousness of others, irrespective of situational and constitutive differences. Conversely, to violate the rule is to fracture the socio-ontological ground of Self and thus metaphysically dis-integrate, become less reflexively conscious and therefore less real to oneself.

In conclusion, some philosophers attempted to improve the Golden Rule by effectively replacing it with the form 'do onto others what is objectively right to do, and be perfectly rational about it' (Gewirth, Alan. The Golden Rule Rationalized. Midwest Studies in Philosophy, 1978, 141). For the rule to do what some philosophers presumed it ought to do we would have to be sufficiently informed about social ontology, normativity and perfectly rational about our intentions, but we are not: "We do not walk around with a set of definite desires about how we want to be treated in various types of situations." (Ibid. Wattles 1996, 166) Moreover, any attempt to detach the rule from irrational intentions would negate its positive psychological effect precisely where rational normative evaluation has already failed. The rule dogmatically invites us to apply a fundamental metanormative principle while simultaneously creating a space for reflexive kinship which in turn mitigates our impulsive, emotionally driven responses. Unlike the Categorical Imperative which rationalises the socio-ontological grounding of conscious agency, the rule works directly on the socio-ontological level, beneath rationality, and can therefore be transformative irrespective of our vague or inchoate desires. The ostensibly deficient Golden Rule may work in practice by cultivating the attitude of moral improvement, whereas analytically demanding moral formulas may be practically accessible only under favourable conditions.

# Trolley Problem

A runaway trolley is speeding down the rail track. There are five people on the track ahead, unable to escape and bound to be killed unless the trolley is redirected to a side track. There is one person lying tied up across the side track. You have the capacity to pull a lever, which will redirect the trolley to the side track. You have two options:

1. Do nothing, in which case the trolley will kill the five people on the main track.

2. Pull the lever, diverting the trolley onto the side track where it will kill one person.

The moral premise that is intuitively assumed by the reader of the trolley problem is that you have the obligation to save any person from dying insofar as you have the capacity to do so, just because they are a person. If the moral premise is valid then the obligation extends to all persons, therefore you also have the obligation to save the one person you would have to kill in order to save the other five, therefore the choice entails a contradiction. In addition to the alleged moral obligation to save any person that we have the capacity to save, we may take into account the moral prohibition against intentional killing. On this extended account, no person among the six individuals involved has a better moral entitlement to be saved than the person on the side track, and every person has the moral entitlement not to be intentionally killed for the benefit of another. More generally, moral duties and prohibitions derive from the moral status of the person and are not negated, diminished or amplified by multiple individuals being in the same situation. The multiplicity does not have a higher moral status than the individual. Dividing people into groups with unequal rights to life, determined on the basis of group-properties or group-circumstances, contradicts the premise that we ought to have equal concern for each person, insofar as personhood entails equal moral status. This argument was originally advanced by John M. Taurek (Should the Numbers Count? Philosophy & Public Affairs, 1977, 293–316). Instead of sorting the six individuals into groups of five and one, as if members of these groups had unequal moral status, we must regard all six individuals as possessing equal rights. It makes no moral difference to the prohibition against intentional killing whether the number of people on the main track are five or one, or zero. In order to maintain logical consistency we must also reject the premise that there is a moral obligation to save lives that conflicts with the moral obligation not to kill intentionally. This conclusion is also consistent with the socially reflexive structure of conscious agency.

We may alternatively apply the Golden Rule to determine whether we would accept a particular solution if we were in the position of any of the individuals involved. It is unlikely that anyone would choose to divert the trolley if they were identified as the person on the side track and expected to be killed as a consequence of their choice. It is also unlikely that many would choose not to divert the trolley if they were identified as one of the persons on the main track and expected to be killed if nothing were done. In regard to the above expectation about preferences, the Golden Rule can be applied by assuming that the decision-maker has equal probability of being identified as a person on the main track or on the side track, and their decision would amount to flipping a coin for their own life. This interpretation approaches the Biblical formula linking the Golden Rule to self-interest: "For with the judgment you pronounce you will be judged, and with the measure you use it will be measured to you."

The trolley problem implies (by omission) that persons are fungible, units of equal and interchangeable value, mutually indifferent, the same, not unique, therefore impersonal, individually dispensable, which conflicts with the presupposition that persons are individually valuable in virtue of their personhood and not just a commodity. Another way, the harm done to X is not 'compensated for' or negated by the benefit to Y, where X and Y are individuals of equal moral status; the harm will always be only a harm to the former and the benefit will always be only a benefit for the latter. The said instances of value are neither of the same kind nor opposition ally equivalent, because they are intrinsically personal and in part unique. For a comprehensive overview of this question see Muñoz, Daniel. Each Counts for One. Philosophical Studies, 2024.

The choice-constraints in the trolley problem are morally rigged and must be rejected. They do not allow the decision-maker to intend to save all six individuals, to treat each individual 'individually' in virtue of their personhood, irrespective of whether this outcome is achievable, or to refuse to make a determination on the terms presented, but the scope of practical intentions cannot be limited by declaring that they are hypothetically limited. The primary moral obligation in any situation is not to intentionally kill anyone and to treat every individual according to their individual moral status.

## Greater Good and Universal Rights

I argued that to do good in the moral sense is to act in any way that is 'consistent with the structure of being'. Conversely, actions that are morally wrong are contrary to the structure of being. In this section I refer to moral properties in terms of good and evil in order to make a distinction between moral and non-moral conceptions of value. Good and evil are binary, mutually exclusive moral properties of intentional action, synonymous with being morally right and morally wrong. Things and states are neither right nor wrong in the moral sense. When we call a thing or state good, we mean that it is valuable and preferable in the utilitarian sense, instrumentally beneficial, which is a matter of degree, more or less useful to our purpose or satisfying our preferences, not that it is the binary opposite of being morally wrong. Conversely, when we call a thing or state bad, we mean that it has negative utility, which is also a matter of degree, more or less detrimental to our purpose or preferences, inferior to other things or states, not that it is the binary opposite of being morally right. The idea of greater good conflates the utilitarian sense of good/better and bad/worse (instrumentally valuable) with the moral sense (right or wrong irrespective of purpose), and thus falsely implies that moral wrongs can be categorised as morally good by virtue of being useful; a category error. The criterion of usefulness or benefits is not a sufficient basis of moral judgement because an action may be useful or beneficial to immoral ends.

The idea of greater good stands in radical opposition to the idea of common good (good for all). The kind of 'good' that trades harms inflicted on some people for the benefit of others is always only good (in the utilitarian sense) for those who benefit and bad for those who suffer the harms. Taking the trolley problem as an example, the one person sacrificed for the benefit of the five is not a beneficiary of the greater good but a victim of murder, which is of itself bad according to the motivational premises of the problem. The concept of greater good is therefore not good to some - the victim - therefore its social generalisation as 'good' is logically inconsistent, therefore false and contrary to the socially reflexive structure of consciousness.

On the most charitable interpretation, the concept of greater good is limited to serving the preferences of some people without causing any harm to others, but even this interpretation entails an is/ought fallacy, purporting to deduce what preferences we ought to serve from whatever preferences we happen to have. Subjective preferences cannot possibly justify our actions or rules, especially when those actions or rules purport to be ethical, because subjective beliefs do not ground a normative principle that dictates the rightness or wrongness of subjective beliefs. Kieran Setiya argues that beliefs explain our reasons but do not normatively justify them: "the standards of practical reason must be ones that we can violate, even in acting for reasons - among other things, they are standards for what we do for reasons - so they could not possibly be satisfied (in every case) just by acting as one intends." (Setiya, Kieran. Explaining Action. The Philosophical Review, 2003, 375) Douglas Lavin reaches a similar conclusion: "There is no normativity if you cannot be wrong." (Lavin, Douglas. Practical Reason and the Possibility of Error. Ethics, 2004, 425) Another way, your preferences cannot be subject to a moral principle if the moral principle is subject to your preferences.

By reducing humans to the status of beneficiaries of interests without regard for the absolute value of conscious agency as the reason for valuing those interests, the entire edifice of utilitarian ethics commits to a contradiction. On the other hand, the calculus of aggregate utility dehumanises conscious agents by regarding them as fungible objects; a commodity instead of fraternity and reflexivity. On both counts, utilitarian ethics negates the normative presupposition of its own value-judgement and, by reflexive implication, abrogates the moral status of the person making the judgement. Without absolute values there is no objective measure of value, therefore no rational basis for the judgement of proportionality, let alone for deriving moral judgement from the judgement of proportionality. "If the moral discourse is lacking, there is no way to demonstrate that values, indeed, are commensurable, and it makes no sense, therefore, to pretend that the principle of proportionality allows us to do it." (Tsakyrakis, Stavros. Proportionality: An assault on human rights? International Journal of Constitutional Law, 2009, 474) Moreover, since the judgement of proportionality is not objectively verifiable but merely posited by those who make it, the judgement is circular and normatively unconstrained, therefore not normative.

The argument from proportionality is typically employed to justify actions or policies that 'limit' human rights (where 'limitation' has the sense of depriving a person of something that persons normally have the right not to be deprived of) for the sake of a politically contingent, ungrounded, vague, unstable and logically inconsistent idea of Greater Good. The overt rationale of this approach is to 'balance' the rights the individual against those of others in the right way, without engaging in the moral discourse about normative premises.

Proponents of the 'principle' of proportionality may argue that when the conventional moral premises expressed in the form of human rights come into conflict, any deeper moral evaluation would be too analytically demanding to be comprehensible and persuasive to the general public, whereas the pretence of 'balancing of interests' allows all three sides to the dispute (including the judiciary) to save face, even if one party is objectively wronged to protect special interests. On this view, the injustice of proportionality is in continuity with the prejudice of culture: it is more likely to be seen as justice because real justice is incomprehensible to prejudiced minds. Nevertheless, real justice in the face of conflicting interests is possible and provable.

One the essentialist view, which is the only view that can consistently support the claim of authority, "human rights are not merely quantities of freedom but protect some basic status of people as moral agents" (Ibid. 490), and therefore can never be justifiably limited. Insofar as human rights are essential to being human, no true conflict between them is possible; it would entail an essential contradiction in the concept of humanity and thus invalidate it. Every disagreement about human rights must therefore be reduced to a conflict between 'claims of right', and what is presented as universal human rights is in fact only a list of claims of right that remain subject to essentialist scrutiny and the validity of each claim may be questioned and potentially refuted.

Universal human rights are normative conventions whose authority is conditional on their consistency with the fundamental laws. When the practical guidance of normative conventions is inconclusive or contradictory, it is the fundamental laws(rather than the claims of right made under the relevant conventions) that must be adhered to for the normative judgment to make sense. One of the conflicting claims of right may violate the laws of sense, whereas the other may be consistent with the laws. Moreover, not all rights are normatively equal; some rights are more grounded than others, being constitutive of the moral status and value of a person, whereas others are only auxiliary limitations that systemically favour the expression of rational consciousness but are not necessary conditions of the moral status of a person. For example, the right to life cannot be partially (let alone 'proportionally') limited, unlike the freedom of movement or the freedom of expression. In all possible circumstances a person is either alive or dead, exists as a conscious agent or does not exist; one cannot be deprived of life or conscious existence in a "balanced" way because the deprivation of life or conscious existence amounts to the cessation of personhood. Another way to put it is that life/existence is (tautologically) 'being', whereas expression and movement are 'doing', and 'being' is a more fundamental property than what that being 'does'. It follows that the right to life has absolute normative priority over political rights.

Crucially, neither the argument from proportionality nor the argument from fundamentality can justify taking away a fundamental human right from one person in order to secure the same right for another; this would not be discrimination on the basis of the normative priority of rights but an unequal treatment of persons, thus contradicting the universal authority and fundamentality of the relevant right. In a hypothetical situation where the continuity of life of one person is in the relationship of inverse dependency with the continuity of life of another, in the sense that one must die for the other to survive, no resolution based on reciprocal claims of the right to life is permissible apart from the prohibition against killing.

A violation 'of the right to life' of a person (or any other right) may occur irrespective of whether that person is deprived 'of life' (or any other property that the relevant right protects). The right to life entails that humans 'may not' be arbitrarily deprived of life. The right is therefore violated by imposing conditions under which a person 'may' be arbitrarily deprived of life, for example, when a person is subject to a mandate that requires participation in an activity due to which a percentage of participants are expected to die. Moreover, the premise that humans may be coerced to accept conditions under which they may be arbitrarily deprived of life implies that humans do not have the right to life on account of being human. The said violation devalues all of humanity, including those who impose and justify the violation, although it may apply to any class of persons and need only have a potential rather than concrete effect on their rights (see, for example, Innes v Electoral Commission of Queensland & Anor (No 2) [2020] QSC 293 at 292).

In regard to the act of intentional killing in self-defence, the recognition of a Human is based not just on rational communication but is primarily phenomenological. If it looks like a human then it is bound to affect us like a human. The threat posed by another can help to rationalise a defensive killing but cannot neutralise the phenomenological effect. All intentional killing, including in self-defence or in defence of others, has a metaphysical cost for the defending agent that is not negated by the reasons for the killing, even if the reasons mitigate the moral consequences. The only moral solution, the only solution that evades the loss of integrity, is to practice self-defence and protection of others with the absolute commitment not to kill intentionally.

The most interesting moral question, in my assessment, is whether a defender who is aware that there are negative metaphysical consequences for intentional killing may still rationally accept those consequences in order to reduce the risk to the lives of others - an act motivated by moral self-sacrifice for the perceived benefit of others. I argue that such self-sacrifice is not in the ultimate interest of others if the net effect on all of humanity is factored into the equation. The act reflexively devalues humanity, including those who are being defended. It is also not necessarily true that intentional killing is the most effective approach to protecting anyone. On a more speculative note, formulated on the basis of personal experience, item may be that when we aim to do what is objectively right, structurally right, the events somehow turn out right, against the apparent odds, as if a more fundamental causal relation were involved, so that acting in synergy with the moral law affected the outcome of events, unveiling new circumstances that modify the problem in unexpected ways. The instance of 'right intention' may be causally significant in itself.

Finally, it may be argued that rights derived from the value of rational consciousness are inherently conditional on the quality of rational consciousness, and if the capacity for rational consciousness is a matter of degree that may vary from person to person, either developed or degraded by individual actions and not determined by external factors, then non-fundamental human rights may be justifiably apportioned unequally, according to the degree of rational consciousness. I contend that any rights that could be rationally limited in this way do not qualify as Human rights since they do not attach to rational consciousness as a matter of principle (which characterises every Human and is inherently imperfect) but as a matter of quality, therefore amount to the rights of the ideal agency (that nobody can live up to). Moreover, variable rights offer no protection from irrational judgements of others about the degree of rational consciousness of a person, nor can they account for any unrealised capacities of persons, which defies the purpose of human rights.

# Part Three: Rules of Meaning

It is uncontroversially true that in order to reliably satisfy our preferences or fulfil our aims we must think consistently, in compliance with the laws of sense. Logical errors corrupt our reasons and result in actions that are conflicted and contrary to self-interest. More critically, the integrity of conscious agency is conditional on the logical consistency of self-conception with respect to the world as we know it, including other beings of the same kind, in accordance with the socially mediated structure of reflexive consciousness.

In this final part I analyse the fundamental laws of logic, their formal implications, common errors, related principles and provide proofs of their interdependence. Nothing else in this book can be consistently interpreted and applied without consistent interpretation and application of the laws of sense.

## Law of identity

The law of identity, one of the fundamental laws of existence, entails that everything is identical (only) to itself. It does not purport to tell us what any particular thing is, but defines the sense-constraint inherent in the concept of identity of a thing that makes any thing meaningful as a thing. The qualifier 'only' is bracketed because it is already implied by the term 'identical', or self-sameness, or =; that which is not itself is necessarily not identical to itself. Every individual, by virtue of being identifiable, implies either constitutive or contextual uniqueness, which is to say, the quality of being a one that is differentiable from every other one, "for it is impossible to think of anything if we do not think of one thing; but if this is possible, one name might be assigned to this thing" (The Complete Works of Aristotle. Princeton: Princeton University Press, 1984, 1006b). "To single x out is to isolate x in experience; to determine or fix upon x in particular by drawing spatio-temporal boundaries and distinguishing it in its environment from other things and unlike kinds..." (Wiggins, David. Sameness and Substance Renewed. 2001, 6) Another way, it is impossible to formulate the law of identity without already applying it, since it is an objective law of meaning itself. The law of identity is fundamental - it is an intrinsic property of meaning or logical sense - we therefore cannot escape the circularity of the law and its application in making sense of the law, but we can express the law more explicitly, as if the symbol of identity (=) did not presuppose it.

If we are able to identify two things (a, b), or two occurrences of a thing, there must be some difference between them, otherwise it would make no sense to say that there are two things, or two occurrences of a thing. It is sufficient for two things to be distinguished only by modal, dispositional or counterfactual properties. If, for example, two or more things were at the same time and in every respect identical, except their spatial location, therefore copies of the same constitution, this would only entail the identity of a 'kind', in which case the relevant kind would be identical 'only to itself' whereas the two copies would not be identical as one-another's 'itself'. Two individuals (a, b) belong to the same kind iff "a has to b the relation of identity as restricted to things that f" (Ibid. Wiggins, 17). Another way, (the same) f is a property or part of both a and b, but a is not absolutely identical to b. This is affirmed by Aristotle as a case of equivalence of a and b with respect to all properties except absolute identity:

"When A belongs to the whole of B and to C and is affirmed of nothing else, and B also belongs to every C, it is necessary that A and B should be convertible; for since A is said of B and C only, and B is affirmed both of itself and of C, it is clear that B will be said of everything of which A is said, except A itself." (Ibid. Aristotle, 68a)

A possible objection to this thesis is that a subatomic particle (x) could hypothetically occupy two spatial locations simultaneously. I contend that the assertion that x is a single particle (or 'the same' particle) implies that it is in fact a simple extended object - an object that occupies a range of locations - therefore a singular identity. Another way, we cannot consistently assert the existence of a single particle in two locations at the same time and also claim that these are two indiscernible particles; we have to commit to the existence of either One particle, in which case it just occupies a range of locations, or to the existence of two particles in different locations (that are related in a special way).

It follows that for anything to have identity it must have a unique identity (therefore discernibility), otherwise it would be unclear which of the objects that ambiguously share their identity is being referred to. This is not equivalent to the case where multiple objects are unambiguously referred to under collective identity, which must in turn be unique as a group, a composite or a kind. The condition of discernibility is not explicitly captured by $\forall x(x=x)$. "[Self-identity] is certainly a relation formally or logically speaking, but it also holds trivially, it's trivially true of everything..." (Strawson, Galen. 'Self-intimation'. Phenomenology and the Cognitive Sciences, 2013)

In contrast, G.E. Moore (Identity. Proceedings of the Aristotelian Society, 1901) argued that the common definition of the law of identity is not trivial but, rather, implicitly contradictory:

"When we say, 'This is identical with itself', the truth of which we are thinking seems to belong to the class of truths of which the general form is, 'This is identical with that', and it seems as if in all such cases 'this' and 'that' must have some difference from one another, and therefore that, in this case, the thing must be different from itself in order to be identical."

The objection raised by Moore and Strawson do not arise once the condition of indiscernibility is taken into account, whereby the meta-language form 'this=that' (an equivocation between the identity of different linguistic terms and what they are intended to identify) is transformed into a strict object-language form 'this=this'. In order to accomplish this result it is necessary to declare uniqueness and therefore singularity of the term in question, which is just what Moore (Ibid.) was concerned about: "The Law of Identity asserts of everything that it belongs to a certain class: let us say, the class of subjects... We want to say not only that it is a subject like other things, but which subject it is."

Consider the following example. There is a reservoir containing 100 tennis balls. A variable ($x$) ranges over 1000 cases of a single ball being drawn. After each draw, the self-identity of the selected ball is noted and the ball is returned to the reservoir. Since the number of choices greatly exceeds the number of physical balls to choose from, we are certain to draw the same ball more than once, but when this occurs the formula ∀x(x=x) does not explicitly relate the present selection to any previous one; it is explicit only insofar as the presently selected ball is identical to itself. In order to express the principle of identity explicitly, as defined by Aristotle, we must include a feature on the basis of which we could be sure, irrespective of how many times we would choose the same ball, irrespective of our capacity to empirically determine whether a particular ball is selected for the second time, that there is only one ball in existence that is identical to this one and it is just this ball.

The formula ∀x(x=x) tells us explicitly that 'everything is identical to itself' which obviously implies that 'nothing is not-identical to itself', but it is neither explicit nor obvious that 'nothing is identical to not-itself': ¬∃x(¬x=x). Uniqueness of identity is only implied by the identity relation (=), but this is also what the formula is intended to express. The fact that there is no scenario in which the sentence 'there is only one ball in existence that is identical to this one, and it is just this ball' is false has no bearing on whether the symbolic expression captures that fact, or whether that fact is explicit and obvious enough not to require a further proof.

The law of identity can be expressed more explicitly as ∀x∃!y(y=x), which translates 'among all things (x) there is only one thing that is identical to any particular thing', or simply 'everything is identical Only to itself'. We can prove this sentence by demonstrating that its negation implies contradiction:

1. ¬∀x∃!y(y=x)
 → ∃x¬∃!y(y=x)
 → ∃x¬∃y(y=x) ∨ ∃x∃y∃z(x=y.x=z.¬y=z)

2. $\exists x \neg \exists y (y=x)$
   $\rightarrow \neg \exists x (x=x)$
   $\rightarrow \forall x (\neg x=x)$
   $\rightarrow \bot$
3. $\exists x \exists y \exists z (x=y . x=z . \neg y=z)$
   $\rightarrow \exists x (\neg x=x)$
   $\rightarrow \bot$
4. $\therefore \neg \forall x \exists! y (y=x)$
   $\rightarrow \bot$

Since first-order logic presupposes the law of non-contradiction, which implies that 'nothing is identical to not-itself' $\neg \exists x (\neg x=x)$, then uniqueness of identity is also one of the theorems of first-order logic, implied by the identity symbol (=). $\forall x (x=x)$ is therefore logically equivalent to $\forall x \exists! y (y=x)$ but it expresses uniqueness of identity only implicitly whereas $\forall x \exists! y (y=x)$ does so explicitly and as such is a more faithful statement of the law of identity as formulated by Aristotle.

## Hegel on identity by double-negation

The law of identity excludes *everything else* by implication of the term 'identical'. Hegel erroneously assumed that self-identity (x=x) does not imply difference from anything else, which resulted in a cascade of false inferences: "If everything is *identical* with itself, then it is not *different*, is not *opposed*, has no *ground*. Or if it is assumed that there are *no two things alike*, that is, that all things are *different* from each other, then A is not equal to A, nor is A in opposition". (Hegel. Science of Logic, 11.260)

The law of identity implies that identity consists in being different from everything else.

This alternative way of formulating the law of identity employs double negation (negation of the negation), signified by the terms 'different' and 'else'; that which is different from everything else is *itself* or the *same*. In eliminating this double negation and rearranging terms we would return to the classical form of the law. We can further formalise the alternative form of the law in a way that approximates Hegel's thesis of the 'unity of identity and difference':

*Identity (of a thing) is identical to difference from everything else.*

The intended sense of the term 'identical' is the logical relation of identity (=):

*Identity (of a thing) = difference from everything else.*

On this interpretation, the term "abstract identity" in Hegel signifies the identity of a thing in relation to other things, or what a thing is, as in 'this is a table', which is different from everything that is not a table, whereas "essential identity" is the logical relation of identity (=/is), as in 'table is a table': "Essence is therefore simple self-identity. This self-identity is the immediacy of reflection. It is not that self-equality which being is, or also nothing, but a self-equality which, in producing itself as unity, does not produce itself over again, as from another, but is a pure production, from itself and in itself, essential identity. It is not, therefore, abstract identity or an identity which is the result of a relative negation preceding it, one that separates indeed what it distinguishes from it but, for the rest, leaves it existing outside it, the same after as before." (SL 11.260)

It is crucial to note that the statement 'x is different from not-x (everything else)' is equivalent to 'x is not not-x', which can be expressed as x = not-not-x. The not-x is logically related to x, indeed constitutively necessary to x insofar as x exists only in relation to not-x, and vice versa. This is not a contradiction, in the sense of not-x and x being identical, in the sense of having the same 'identity' or being true in the same respect, as erroneously concluded by Hegel, but has the sense of the law of identity: x = x is equivalent to x = not-not-x, which is equivalent to not-x = not-x. Hegel was evidently either not aware or did not accept the logical equivalence of these forms: "each [thing] is self-unlike and contradictory in its equality with itself, and each self-identical in its difference, in its contradiction: that everything intrinsically is this movement of transition of one of these determinations to the other, and that everything is this transition because each determination is itself, within it, the opposite of itself." (SL 11.261) "All things are in themselves contradictory." (SL 11.286)

It could be argued that Hegel's notion of "contradiction" is a misnomer, not a formal contradiction, since it is 'resolved/sublated' at the meta-level, or what Hegel calls "ground" (SL 11.280-83), which amounts to a distinction of logical types: 1) identities of the relata; 2) identity of the relation between the relata. Another way, the relation of difference is logically distinct from the relation of identity. The difference/opposition between the relations of identity and difference is a relation of a higher order (different logical type). That relation has an identity in its own right, to which the opposites belong (as parts) without being identical with the meta-relation (the whole) or with one another. Every identity is related to all other identities, by virtue of being different from them.

The Hegelian notion of the 'unity' of identity and difference is therefore at best trivial, applicable to everything and always, because everything is constitutively related in the realm of meaning, every word is defined by all other words, every object is related to all other objects in space and time. In this sense, Hegelian 'unity' is just the property of being in the same world; it neither complements nor transcends the law of identity. Otherwise, it amounts to a negation of all meaning.

## The meaning of 1

One(1) is the numerical analogue of identity and the most basic application of the law of identity - one of the fundamental laws of logic, which states that everything is identical only to itself and therefore different from everything else. All other numbers are multiples, sets, fractions, or functions of the identity-type signified by One; for example, number 4 represents a basic set of units of a certain size: {1,1,1,1}. "For each number is said to be many because it consists of ones and because each number is measurable by one..." (Ibid. Aristotle, 1057a) The law of identity dictates a distinction between specific identity (this one) and the identity-type (any one). For example, the identity-type 'apple' that all specific apples belong to is also a specific identity in its own right, but only as a type (an identity/unity of a higher order), which is different from the identities/unities that belong to it (the first order or basic identities). By making the type distinction, consistency/sense is maintained in relation to the identity of each unit, uniquely positioned and counted in a set, or any unit belonging to the set, or for the count of sets and supersets (sets of sets).

A thing is intrinsically a one identity, a unity. "A unit is that by virtue of which each of the things that exist is called one." (Euclid, and T. L. Heath. Euclid's Elements (Volume II). Cambridge University Press, 1908, 278) One-ness is synonymous with identity, with the conceptual integrity of a meaningful whole, uniquely differentiable from every other meaningful whole. As such, the count as one is the metaphysical essence of meaning and therefore of all conceivable being, of being itself as oneself (1=1). Simultaneously, one-ness is logically compatible with parthood, where each part is itself a whole of a different kind, a one/unitary identity at the level of fractions, differentiable from the identity of the whole at the level to which it belongs as a part.

Arithmetic operations signify various methods of counting ones. For example, the multiplier is the count of singular sets of the same size (each with the same count of members), whereas the multiplicand is the count of singular members in each set; the dividend is the count of singular members of all the sets comprising a superset, whereas a divisor is the count of the sets, each with the same count of members. The elementary equation 2+2=4 is coherent and therefore meaningful, irrespective of being true or false in any other sense, because 2 is counted as equal to (which has the sense of being 'identical with' and therefore having the 'identity of') 1+1, and 4 is equal to 1+1+1+1, so that 1+1+1+1=1+1+1+1, which is in turn reducible to 1=1, to a self-reflexive unity. One is its own power and root. Any number multiplied by one is itself; anyone multiplied by one is oneself. Oneness is the logical equivalent of a mirror, where any operation by means of one reproduces the operand on the other side of the equation, thereby formalising the symmetry of identity (=).

On the other hand, one meter [m] (unit of length) is distinct from one second [s] (unit of time), which is in turn distinct from one kilogram [kg] (unit of mass), but the distinction is subsumed in the implication of all three units in the unit of force: Newton $[N] = [kg.m/s^2]$. It is only because of this implication at a higher level of unity that distinct qualities (time, mass, length and force) are ontologically compatible, physically meaningful, which is to say, co-exist in the same world. It follows that there is nothing in our field of experience that does not already belong in common to some category (identity-type).

Ontological implications of oneness are not trivial, for if to exist as one is to be related to other ones, every identity being meaningful only in a relationally coupled world-context, then all identities are necessarily determined by their relations with one another. In that sense, all co-existents are only complex, reflexive relations of multiplicity, with no fundamental referents or relata that can be identified among the existents. Badiou argued that "The multiple from which ontology makes up its situation is composed solely of multiplicities. There is no one." (Badiou, Alain. Being and Event. Continuum, 2005. 29) This is true if understood in the same sense as Russell's paradox (that the totality cannot be consistently thought of as one), but this negative thesis is not logically satisfying as an explanation of that which positively 'is', or is identifiable, meaningful, conceivable, relatable, even only as a relation or a synthesis of multiple relations. The proposition that one/identity cannot 'exist' without multiplicity is not equivalent to nor does it imply that 'there is no one'. The one is both the logical structure of meaning and being (the law of identity) and its only content (that which is identified and can be related to); meaning and being is conceivable neither as content without the structure that 'makes it' identifiable nor as a pure structure, without any identifiable content, but only in the reflexive distribution/repetition of itself (reflexive plurality).

The entanglement of the logical structure and its content has normative significance for conscious agents. If all the identifiable instances of conscious agency are determined by their reflexive relations with all other instances of conscious agency, then ethics is inseparable from ontology, with existential consequences for disrupting social reflexivity, whereby the oneness, the unity, therefore the identity of Self is negated and its being degraded.

## Law of non-contradiction and its relationship to identity and excluded middle

There are three classical formulations of the law of non-contradiction:

1. A proposition cannot be true and false at the same time and in the same respect.

2. An attribute cannot at the same time belong and not belong to the same thing in the same respect.

3. A meaning/sense and its negation cannot be expressed in the same thought or be simultaneously intended for action.

The first (*semantic*) formulation is grounded in the concept of truth, which implies consistency of all true propositions. (Ibid. Aristotle, 1011b13-14)

The second (*ontological*) formulation is grounded in what can be meaningfully attributed to the same identity. It is impossible to identify anything in terms of attributes without respecting the law of non-contradiction in regard to the attributes. (Ibid. Aristotle, 1005b19–20)

The third (*doxatic*) formulation is grounded in the integrity/unity of thought. It is impossible to think a thought that both affirms and denies the same meaning. A statement that affirms and denies the same meaning has no meaning beyond the incompatibility of its parts, which are two successive thoughts of which one must be denied for the other to be meaningful. (Ibid. Aristotle,1005b24-25)

The relationship between the law of non-contradiction and the law of identity can be formulated as follows:

$\forall x \neg(x \land \neg x)$
$\rightarrow \forall x \neg(T(x)=T(\neg x))$
$\rightarrow \forall x(T(x)=T(x))$
$\rightarrow \forall x(x=x)$

For all x, x and not-x cannot both be true (i.e. cannot have the same truth-value), which implies that the truth-value of x is equal/identical to the truth-value of x, which can be expressed as x is equal/identical to x.

The relationship between the law of identity and the law of excluded middle can be formulated as follows:

$\forall x(x=x)$
$\rightarrow \neg\exists x(\neg x=x)$
$\rightarrow \forall x \neg \exists y(y=\neg x \land y=x)$
$\rightarrow \forall x \neg \exists y \neg(\neg(y=\neg x) \lor \neg(y=x))$
$\rightarrow \forall x \neg\neg(\neg\neg x \lor \neg x)$
$\rightarrow \forall x(x \lor \neg x)$

The law of identity implies that there can be no third term that is neither x nor not-x, since the third term implies identity of x and not-x, therefore non-identity of x. The law of identity implies the law of excluded middle.

The law of excluded middle can be proven by deriving contradiction from the negation of excluded middle:

$\neg\forall x(x \lor \neg x)$
$\rightarrow \exists x \exists y(y \rightarrow \neg(x \lor \neg x))$
$\rightarrow \exists x \exists y(y \rightarrow (\neg x \land \neg\neg x))$
$\rightarrow \exists x(\neg x \land x)$
$\rightarrow \bot$

The negation of the law of excluded middle implies a term y that is neither x nor not-x, therefore y implies both not-x and not-not-x, therefore contradiction. The law of excluded middle is implied by the law of non-contradiction, which closes the loop of interdependence of the three fundamental laws.

# Principle of explosion

The principle of explosion is a logical rule according to which 'from contradiction anything follows' (*ex contradictione sequitur quodlibet*), including its negation. In this section I discuss the implications of the principle vis-a-vis non-classical logics.

The principle is commonly proven in the following way:

1. Assume that 'P is true'.

2. Assume that 'P is not true' is also true.

(1 and 2 imply the rejection of the law of non-contradiction.

3. Introduce C = 'P is true OR unicorns exist'. 'P is true' (from 1) implies that C is true irrespective of whether unicorns exist.

4. C and 'P is not true' (from 2) imply that unicorns exist.

Formally:

$P \land \neg P: P \rightarrow P \lor Q, (P \lor Q) \land \neg P \rightarrow Q$

The proof attempts to comply with the law of non-contradiction at every step except the truth-value of P, but since Q can be any proposition whatsoever, even a contradiction, any contradiction is also implicitly proven. The proof also contradicts the logical theorems (=, ∧, ∨, →) necessary to construct the proof, therefore negates itself. The meaning of 'from contradiction anything follows' must be taken absolutely: 'from contradiction everything follows, including the negation of everything', therefore no distinction of identity is possible, therefore no meaning. Another way, from contradiction, nonsense follows.

To formalise this result explicitly one could modify C: 'P is true OR (everything is true AND everything is not true)'.

It is impossible to circumvent any of the fundamental laws (identity, non-contradiction, excluded middle) and retain the capacity for meaning. This can be demonstrated in several ways, but the demonstration may prioritise the law of identity: everything is identical to itself and only to itself. Without adhering to the law of identity, nothing could be said to be itself or a definite something, therefore no identification of objects, meanings, relations or terms would be possible. Furthermore, the law of identity entails that nothing can be both identical and not identical to itself (the law of non-contradiction) and nothing can be partly identical or partly non-identical to itself (the law of excluded middle). To reject non-contradiction or excluded middle amounts to implicitly rejecting identity/=, therefore to reject any of the laws amounts to rejecting them all.

Proponents of paraconsistent logic attempt to circumvent the law of non-contradiction, claiming that classical logic is not fit for effective reasoning under the realistic conditions of vagueness, ambiguity and uncertainty. This view appears to be motivated by misinterpretation of classical logic and is typically exemplified as equivocation between incompatibility (statements that are mutually exclusive but need not be held true at the same time and in the same respect) and contradiction (true and false at the same time and in the same respect). For example, that Newtonian physics and General Relativity yield different predictions for the same system does not entail a contradiction; difference, ambiguity, uncertainty, vagueness, incompatibility or opposition do not of themselves violate the law of non-contradiction. It is possible to consistently 'work' with incompatible propositions in 'classical' logic provided they are not both regarded as true at the same time and in the same respect; the law of non-contradiction is preserved by means of exclusive disjunction (x ORR ¬x), while remaining uncertain which hypothesis is true, instead of x AND ¬x being presumed true because of uncertainty, which is a non sequitur. We can construct paradoxes in 'classical' logic as problems that are yet to be consistently solved, hidden relations to be revealed, rather than accept them as contradictory 'solutions', let alone as true statements about 'contradictory reality', which, as demonstrated above, amounts to nihilism about identity.

Some logics may be only superficially non-classical but are fully consistent with the fundamental laws in their meaningful application (Preservationism). Others (Dialetheism) maintain that the Liar paradox is an example of a 'true contradiction'. Like all paradoxes, "This sentence is false" is a meaningless expression. The law of identity is violated by equivocating between the identity of the sentence "This sentence is false" and the word "sentence" preceded by the word "This". It can be demonstrated that these two instances of 'sentence' are not the same identity, therefore no contradiction occurs. In fact, the term "This sentence" does not refer to anything at all: substitution of the whole sentence for every recurrent instance of "This sentence" results in infinite regress and in an empty subject: "(((((...) is false) is false) is false)...)". It cannot be completed.

Crucially, there can be no meaningful conversation with someone who rejects any of the fundamental laws. Their statements cannot be interpreted to mean what they are normally taken to mean since they could also be intended to mean the opposite, or something altogether different. Someone who rejects any of the laws of sense cannot be understood; their speech has no meaning, they renounce their own voice.

*"To be and not to be, that is and is not the question"...*

## Principle of sufficient reason

Assertions of facts are typically used to express commitments to possibilities that are not necessarily true. We may be practically justified in making assumptions about facts (as possibilities that could be false), but we are not justified in asserting that a particular possibility is true (a fact) without a sufficient reason; this would imply not only that the possibility is true but that we know (with certainty) that the possibility is true. I will show that the latter, second-order claim violates the law of non-contradiction, and is therefore necessarily false as an assertion of knowledge about facts.

The principle of sufficient reason can be expressed as follows: for every fact F, there must be a reason R that implies F. The condition of implication is necessary to avoid triviality; any reason that need not imply would be sufficient of every fact. Now let F signify the knowledge that P is true. It follows that the knowledge that P is true obtains only by virtue of a reason R that implies the knowledge that P is true. A sufficient reason implies the knowledge that P is true, which precludes the possibility that P is false, which can be satisfied only by a proof that P is true.

The law of non-contradiction entails that P cannot be true and false at the same time and in the same respect. To assert that 'P is true' without a sufficient reason implies that 'P is true without a sufficient reason', therefore any claim can be true without a sufficient reason, therefore the negation of P can also be true without a sufficient reason, therefore contradiction. In short, any assertion of fact that violates the principle of sufficient reason, insofar as it is asserted with conviction but without a proof, is self-negating.

This conclusion has special significance for moral theory: a normative principle or judgement has authority only if it is logically provable, therefore imperative, therefore objective, and only a proven principle or judgement can be asserted with authority. It follows that no contingent rule or opinion, irrespective of the 'legitimisation process', may be asserted or enforced with authority.

The principle of sufficient reason must be respected in all logical evaluation because to disregard it is to violate the law of non-contradiction, resulting in nonsense. It also follows from the above that logical consistency entails soundness, a priori invalidating any internally consistent but false arguments; soundness is necessarily logical, and the absence of soundness is nonsensical.

## Law of excluded middle

The law of excluded middle is one of three fundamental laws of thought discovered by Aristotle. It can be expressed informally as follows: for a statement to be meaningful it must be either true or false, or be composed of parts that are either true or false. Formally, this is written (P∨¬P). The law is disputed in the context of many-valued logics, where rejection of the law is thought to be a concession necessary for certain applications. I argue that many-valued logics need not and must not violate the law of excluded middle, as the relevant concession involves an incorrect interpretation of the law.

In the words of Aristotle (Metaphysics, 1011b), "there cannot be an intermediate between contradictories, but of one subject we must either affirm or deny any one predicate." Aristotle clarifies that this does not relate to properties or differences which are only nominally regarded as opposite, for example black/white, with the intermediate terms being shades of grey (Ibid.), but only to a special category of formal contradictories such as true/false or exist/not-exist (De Interpretatione, 9): "if every affirmation or negation is true or false it is necessary for everything either to be the case or not to be the case." In case of natural properties, which are simply differences, irrespective of whether we regard them as contradictory or whether there is a range of steps between them, we must either affirm or deny any one property, be it white, black, or any particular shade of grey. As such, classical logic accepts only two truth-values (true or false). There are cases where it is impossible to determine whether something is true or false, but not knowing the truth-value of something does not entail an additional truth-value (at least not a truth-value of the same type), just like the absence of something (a predicate) does not have the same logical structure as 'the presence of absence' (a predicate of a predicate). When we speak of a something having two possible logical predicates, we speak an object-language (or base-language), that is, the object of a sentence is distinct from the predicates in terms of which we speak about the object; when we speak in terms of predicates about a predicate we speak a meta-language, where meta-predicates refer to predicates from the object-level (base) in the logical hierarchy.

Integrating different types of truth-values to get a quasi-intermediate result can be useful in some circumstances, but does not negate the law of excluded middle: at every level of the logical hierarchy the law of excluded middle strictly applies. Any system of logic that posits intermediate truth values, relates a degree of uncertainty 'about' predicates (a higher order predicate) to the base predicates (true/false), thereby allowing for their relation to be quantified without inconsistency. This is possible (without creating another inconsistency)only insofar as the relation between non-binary truth values is understood as belonging to the meta-language and does not constitute a relation between terms of the binary object-language (true or false); anything else would be a category mistake. "Recognizing a type-distinction is always a way of disallowing exceptions to the Law of Excluded Middle." (Geach, P. T., and W. F. Bednarowski. Symposium: The Law of Excluded Middle. Proceedings of the Aristotelian Society, 1956)

It may be further argued that any violation of the law of excluded middle negates the system of logic that purports to evade it. When a theory identifies an object or a property (P), it is implicitly asserting the law of identity: there exists only one P that in every respect is identical with P. If the theory allows P to neither fully exist nor not-exist, then whatever exists is not identical with P, therefore not-P. Alternatively, if the degree of existence of P is different from the degree of existence of Q and there are no other differences between them, then P and Q are not identical in 'every respect', therefore not 'identical'. It is not conceivable for P to be less real or less true than itself.

As a possible challenge to the above argument let us posit something called P-ness: a property that can vary in degree, for example, transparency. For the law of identity to hold we cannot say that a homogenous object P has a range of P-ness, unless we just mean that P is identical to the range of P-ness, which is then trivially true of P-ness. We must instead posit the range of P-ness as a property that is distinct from P, which, at time t, can have only a definite amount and distribution of P-ness. If we can identify P with a definite degree of P-ness, then we must say that P with a definite degree of P-ness either exists or does not exist. The same can be said in terms of predicates 'true' and 'false': that 'a specific degree of true-P is true' is at best a tautology, or it conflates two different meanings of 'true', one being a matter of degree, the other binary.

In *Principia Mathematica* (1910) at *2.1, Whitehead and Russell formulated the canonical proof of the law of excluded middle from the definition of implication at *1.01 ($p \rightarrow q = \neg p \lor q$) and the indispensable 'principle of identity' at *2.08 ($p \rightarrow p$). If 'p implies q' necessitates either not-p or q, then by applying the above definition to $p \rightarrow p$ yields $p \rightarrow p = \neg p \lor p$ and thus necessitates the law of excluded middle.

The law of excluded middle can be alternatively proven by showing that contradiction is a consequence of the negation of excluded middle:

$\neg\forall x(x \lor \neg x)$
→ $\exists x \exists y(y \to \neg(x \lor \neg x))$
→ $\exists x \exists y(y \to (\neg x \land \neg\neg x))$
→ $\exists x(\neg x \land x)$
→ $\bot$

The negation of the law of excluded middle implies a term y that is neither x nor not-x, therefore y implies both not-x and not-not-x, therefore contradiction. The law of excluded middle is implied by the law of non-contradiction.

The intuitionist school of logic, which rejects the law of the excluded middle, may object that the above proof involves 'double negation elimination' ($\neg\neg x \to x$), a principle that the intuitionists also reject. This is not a serious obstacle, since the proof can be constructed in a way that avoids double negation elimination. We can simply regard $\neg x$ as a variable in its own right, such that $\neg x = z$, in which case $y \to (z \land \neg z)$, therefore still contradiction.

$\neg\forall x(x \lor \neg x)$
→ $\exists x \exists y(y \to \neg(x \lor \neg x))$
→ $\exists x \exists y(y \to (\neg x \land \neg\neg x)).\exists z(\neg x = z)$
→ $\exists z(z \land \neg z)$
→ $\bot$

The law of excluded middle remains one of the fundamental laws of logic, indispensable to construction of meaning or logical sense, and the several formal systems purporting to evade this law are a result of its incorrect application, interpreting statements of object- and meta-language as objects of the same logical type. This does not imply that the affected systems are necessarily inconsistent, but only that insofar as they are consistent they do not violate the law of excluded middle despite ostensibly rejecting it.

## Rules of inference

The fundamental laws of logic are the absolute limits of sense, therefore also the limits of inference. The rules of inference depend on the fundamental laws but are not themselves fundamental; they are secondary forms that comply with the laws and are intended to formalise the sense of 'implication'. The logical asymmetry of implication can be characterised in terms of identity: we can interpret 'P implies Q' as analogous to 'Q is a part of P', which is not identical to 'P is a part of Q', except where P is identical to Q. The rules of inference were devised to avoid conflating these logical relations.

Modus Ponens and Modus Tollens are the formal principles of inference (affirmation or denial) by logical implication, universally regarded as valid forms of argument. It is common for these formal principles to be misapplied in natural languages, and some errors of inference are not easy to discern. In this section I examine the most notorious error of practical inference, which is nevertheless not explained in encyclopaedic sources.

Modus Ponens is also referred to as Affirming the Antecedent (P), and Modus Tollens as Denying the Consequent (Q). The property of implication (P implies Q) is formally expressed as 'if P, then Q': if P is true then Q is necessarily true.

Modus Ponens: If P, then Q. P is true. Therefore, Q is true.

*If it is raining, the ground is wet. It is raining. Therefore, the ground is wet.*

Modus Tollens: If P, then Q. Q is false. Therefore, P is false.

*If it is raining, the ground is wet. The ground is not wet. Therefore, it is not raining.*

Modus Ponens and Tollens are not logically reversible, in that making inferences from the consequent (Q) to the antecedent (P) can be false: arguments that initiate from affirming the consequent (AC) or denying the antecedent (DA) are formal logical fallacies.

AC (fallacy of the converse): If P, then Q. Q is true. Therefore, P is true.

*If it is raining, the ground is wet. The ground is wet. Therefore, it is raining.*

DA (fallacy of the inverse): If P, then Q. P is false. Therefore, Q is false.

*If it is raining, the ground is wet. It is not raining. Therefore, the ground is not wet.*

Modus Ponens and Tollens being recognised as valid forms of argument implies that there is no P or Q for which the forms of argument fail. Let us construct an argument based on the Tollens form, by substituting for P and Q as indicated below.

P: an *animal eats a sufficient amount of food to sustain its vital functions*

Q: *the animal survives*

*If an animal eats a sufficient amount of food to sustain its vital functions, then the animal survives. The animal is dead. Therefore, the animal did not eat a sufficient amount of food to sustain its vital functions.*

The cause of the animal dying could be a disease, even if the animal ate enough food throughout its life, therefore the argument is false and Modus Tollens appears to fail.

Another example:

P: *the bomb is disarmed*

Q: *the city is still standing*

*If the bomb were disarmed, the city would still be standing. The city is not standing. Therefore, the bomb was not disarmed.*

The cause of the city not standing could be an earthquake, even if the bomb was disarmed, therefore the argument is false and Modus Tollens appears to fail.

Are these arguments valid counter-examples (therefore refutations) of Modus Tollens? Think about it before continuing to read...

The arguments above are not correct counter-examples of Modus Tollens, but this conclusion is not obvious, since the formally proven formula for Tollens is ostensibly adhered to. The error lies in the use of the term 'if', which means (both in formal logic and in natural languages) that P is a 'sufficient condition' of Q. Going back to the first example, it is not a sufficient condition of survival to eat a sufficient amount of food for survival; it is a 'necessary condition' of survival but not sufficient to guarantee survival. Modus Ponens/Tollens apply a strict logical interpretation of 'if' (sufficiency), as opposed to 'only if' (necessity), and only then Modus Tollens follows logically from Modus Ponens, because the reverse of sufficiency is necessity: 'if P then Q' implies 'only if Q then P'. This last point is also not obvious, so here is an example: if rain is a sufficient condition of the ground being wet, then the ground being wet is a necessary consequence of rain (a water hose could also make the ground wet, but the ground cannot be not wet if it rains). Another way, if it were raining then the ground would be wet, but only if the ground were wet that it could be raining. The meaning of the two conditional expressions ('if' and 'only if') is clearly different.

The above example demonstrates that it is not enough to rely of Modus Ponens and Modus Tollens for consistent reasoning, because these principles are not fundamental. All reasoning is ultimately reducible to the law of non-contradiction (or identity), and the implicit equivocation between 'sufficiency' and 'necessity' involves a contradiction. We can alternatively express sufficiency and necessity in terms of ontological identity, which is arguably the most intuitive foundation of Modus Ponens and Modus Tollens. Assuming that P and Q are not identical or otherwise conditionally equivalent (which is an exception to the rule):

A) 'Q is a part of P' entails 'if P then Q' and 'only if Q then P';

B) 'P is a part of Q' entails 'if Q then P' and 'only if P then Q';

$\neg(P \Leftrightarrow Q): A \wedge B$
$\rightarrow \neg(P=P) \vee \neg(Q=Q)$
$\rightarrow \neg P \vee \neg Q$

Provided that P and Q are not conditionally equivalent, the fallacy of the converse and the fallacy of the inverse are analogous to applying the entailments of B to A, thus affirming both A and B and violating the law of identity. Alternatively, the theorem '$\neg(P \Leftrightarrow Q)$ and if P then Q' is logically equivalent to 'only if Q then P', therefore the logical identity of the two expressions is maintained.

To avoid violating the fundamental laws, the false counter-examples may be re-written by emphasising that P is a necessary condition of Q, rather than (falsely) a sufficient condition:

*An animal can survive **only if** it eats a sufficient amount of food to sustain its vital functions. The animal is dead, but starvation is not the only possible cause of death (the animal died of disease).*

***Only if** the bomb were disarmed, the city would still be standing. The city is not standing, but the bomb was not necessarily the cause of destruction (an earthquake was).*

These corrected expressions do not fit the form of Modus Ponens/Tollens, therefore they are not valid counter-examples of the formal principle: the identity of implication.

The only valid exception to the rule is the case of conditional equivalence (P⇔Q), involving both sufficiency and necessity of P for Q, which works both ways: 'if and only if P then Q' is logically equivalent to 'if and only if Q then P'.

For an in-depth analysis of conditionality in Modus Ponens and Modus Tollens see Ri, Yong-Sok's "Modus Ponens and Modus Tollens: Their Validity/Invalidity in Natural Language Arguments", Studies in Logic, Grammar and Rhetoric 50, no.1 (2017): 253-267.

All valid rules of inference can be reduced to the fundamental laws of sense on the basis of which their validity is determined. Similarly to Modus Ponens and Modus Tollens, De Morgan's laws can also be interpreted in terms of identity. If 'A is true and B is true' constitutes a theorem, and the theorem is negated, and the law of identity dictates that the theorem and its negation are not identical, then it is logically necessary that either A is false or B is false. Alternatively, the negation of the theorem 'A is false or B is false' is logically equivalent to (identical with) the theorem 'A is true and B is true'. Similarly if 'A is true or B is true' constitutes a theorem, and the theorem is negated, then it is logically necessary that both A is false and B is false; every other possibility is logically equivalent (identical with) the theorem. The failure to comply with De Morgan's laws would imply that the theorem and its negation are identical, which would violate the law of identity (and the law of non-contradiction). Every valid logical rule is an analogue of the law of identity, reducible to $x=x$.

## Structure of knowledge

In this final sanction I address the most notorious and possibly the most socially damaging logical error, of which all humans are unwittingly guilty to various degrees. All cultural, political and legal systems that were ever devised are replete with false assertions of knowledge. Knowledge is always simultaneously 'about' something (its object - that which is known) and subject to certain conditions at the meta-level (the conditions of knowing). At the meta-level we can identify three critical terms:

1. *Meaning*: a reference to identity that complies with the law of identity (discernibility).

2. *Truth*: a proposition consisting of multiple meanings expressed in relation to one another that is logically consistent and cannot be contradicted by any other true proposition.

3. *Reality*: the meaning-content of true propositions about causes and effects.

Truth is necessarily consistent with everything that involuntarily affects us (reality), whereas falsity is necessarily inconsistent with it. We can thus distinguish any consistent but false propositions from true propositions by virtue of consistency with the involuntary effects we experience.

Knowledge is commonly conceived of as a property that satisfies the description 'justified true belief'. I argue that the formula 'justified true belief' is necessarily a compound property that entails a logical structure consisting of a simple belief (X) - a truth-claim - and a higher-order true belief (X') that the simple belief is true - the truth-maker. The higher-order true belief that X is certainly true can be satisfied only by a proof. If I am not certain that X is true, on the basis of certainty entailing reasons, then I am not justified in categorically asserting the knowledge that X is true and thus implicitly denying the known possibility that X is false. For claims of fact based on a known 'probability' one must affirm the degree of uncertainty, which is necessary to determine the weight of the probabilistic justification for the claim. For example, if the proven probability that X is true is 99%, the true second-order belief is not 'X is true' but 'the probability that X is true is 99%'. The hypothetical belief that $P(X)=99\%$ implies 'X is true' is provably false (the law of identity).

The key to the problem is to recognise that knowledge is a state of reflexive consciousness and as such necessarily involves two logical types of referents: the subject and the object of belief. The higher-order referent constitutes the distinction between simple believing (in object-level truths) vs. knowledge, which includes the awareness of the scope and quality of justification that the conscious subject has access to (the meta-level of rational justification). It does not suffice, on pain of contradiction, to have just any justification for claiming knowledge, since every possible belief can be supported by reasons in an inconclusive way, including contradictory beliefs (the principle of sufficient reason). Knowledge requires the possession of a truth-maker, not just a possibility-maker.

The logical conditions of knowledge can be formulated as follows:

A) a falsifiable simple belief that X is true (where X can signify the probability of Y);

B) the awareness of conditions (truth-makers) on account of which 'A is certainly true'; OR

A') a falsifiable simple belief that X is uncertain (where X can signify the probability of Y);

B') the awareness of conditions (truth-makers) on account of which 'A is certainly true'.

Crucially, AB and A'B' constitute different categories of knowledge; AB can be non-trivially true, whereas A'B' is always trivially true (as the knowledge of unquantified uncertainty, which applies to every unproven claim).

I have provisionally identified only two types of truths that can be known:

1) logically necessary truths (*a priori*), which can be proven to hold for given premises, which may themselves be only hypothetical (need not be proven);

2) truths of the record (*a posteriori*), which can be proven by correspondence to the linguistic or numerical content of the record, irrespective of whether the content is true in any other respect.

Our capacity for knowledge is limited to information that is logically necessary or recorded and verifiable against the record.

Every instance of human perception is subjective, unique and contingent in its description, so to extract 'data' of a particular type, perceptions (observations) have to be idealised and homogenised according to abstract categories that are distinct from the categories of objects that we already 'naively' experience. Those abstract categories are theoretically invented, and by doing so we extend or extrapolate our conception of reality in a creative way. Perceptions are thereby standardised as measurements and provisionally validated on the basis of logical coherence, temporal correlation and ontological continuity with other idealised terms that are relevant to the standard. The process of experimental replication of the standardised meaning 'in the data' reapplies the same type of idealisation to our 'naive' or 'native' perceptions of 'the world as we know it' in order to validate the process. We call this process empirical science. Empirical science relies on a priori truths to produce 'truths of the record' of its conceptual standardisation.

No amount of data that fits a theory can prove the theory or any inductive claim about objective reality. It is not possible to know by means of the scientific method what will happen in the future or the probabilities of future events; we can only know the probabilities that follow a priori from the recorded data, which is already a form of creative idealisation about the past and tells us nothing about future data, about the meaning of other possible types of data, and whether the phenomenological idealisations inherent in the data are meaningful and informative about objective reality or do they only reflect something internal to consciousness that has no objective 'outside'. This raises the question: what is the actual object that empirical sciences study? What is science for if it cannot 'know' the world we experience? We can infer from the scientific praxis that it is essentially focussed on making a priori statistical deductions from a given set of homogenised information, but that information is unprovable and not truth-apt, since it is based on subjective, naive observations that are themselves unprovable and not truth-apt. We do not 'know' whether we are using 'the same' way of measuring 'the same' phenomenon, we merely agree that we do. "This is connected with the fact that no part of our experience is at the same time a priori. Whatever we see could be other than it is. Whatever we can describe at all could be other than it is. There is no a priori order of things." (Wittgenstein, Ludwig. Tractatus Logico-Philosophicus. Routledge & Kegan Paul, 1974, 5.634) On the other hand, "a thought is a proposition with a sense." (Ibid. 4) Every phenomenal experience (perception) is also an instance of sense, intrinsically structured according to the laws of sense: the universal meta-language we *know* insofar as anything makes sense to us as a definite something 'being there' or 'appearing'. This knowledge is intersubjectively affirmed by the intention to communicate a sense to others and is presupposed in the use of language (cf. Ibid. 3.334). Based on this universal constant, common to all conscious agents, a range of logical properties can be deduced a priori from the idealised content of experience, which may be broadly characterised as 'count' and 'measure'. These meta-physical properties are the proper object of science.

Scientific rigour does not eliminate the subjectivity of the original perceptions of studied phenomena or the secondary perception of abstracting those original perceptions into data. Evidential statements about subjective experiences are subjective ascriptions, which are not objectively normative: "whereas there are objective facts about objective disagreement, there are no objective facts about subjective disagreement, only objective facts about subjective disagreement ascriptions" (Bob Beddor, *Subjective Disagreement.* Nous, 2018, 25). Ascriptions about the meaning of subjective experiences have the function of suggesting a normative description for a particular phenomenological context. When the a priori scientific deductions from the propositional ascriptions are reliably reproduced from multiple subjective sources of homogenised 'data', the underlying theory possesses a degree of ascriptional conformity and therefore a phenomenological foundation of a new technology. At this point the scientific theory is deemed valid, not in the sense of a logical truth but on account of satisfying a consensus-based, procedural standard of validity, which is itself unprovable. Another way, scientific concepts and inferences internal to a theory about 'the world as we know it' may exhibit sufficient systemic coherence with other scientific concepts, which renders the theory scientifically (but not logically) valid. In this sense, science and technology are a semi-formal 'object-language', a ritual we design and act out to mediate our will via a newly generalised sense of experience in the world as we know it, whose systemic meaning is also progressively modified by this type of communication. Science, when done with procedural consistency, can be realised as technology, can be engineered to have a physical effect, and together they constitute two sides of a logically systematised, ritual phenomenology, augmenting the sense of reality rather than discovering something that was always already real: a phenomenological machine.

Ascriptional conformity applies to everything in the empirical domain, but there is a difference in the level of phenomenological grounding of our agreement on 'what' is there between scientific constructs and naive constructs. We interact with naive objects intimately in terms of 'what they are like', we have deep associations about 'likeness' and can easily describe and compare things to other things, which are also 'like' something else, which makes for a highly integrated system of associations (type-equivalences). Science, for the most part, does not work like this. Instead it posits abstractions that are phenomenologically not like anything we experience at all. We have no idea what Caesium pulses feel like, we cannot tell them apart from nothingness, we do not know what an ampere of electric current or a joule of energy is 'like', so science uses metaphors and visual fictions to give us a vague sense of what the abstraction ought to be like. The scientific abstractions can be made 'real' only be converting them into the ritual of technology, an instrument or a machine, and persuading the general public that the ritual expresses precisely those scientific concepts. The scientific-technological paradigm thus presents a more aggressive demand for faith than naive experience, and its mode of conversion to believe in the Theory (a kind of Supernatural) is based on submission to power, mediated as ritual, not on knowledge, which resonates with the anthropological observations of Mircea Eliade about ritual 'knowledge':

"In general it can be said that myth, as experienced by archaic societies, (1) constitutes the History of the acts of the Supernaturals; (2) that this History is considered to be absolutely *true* (because it is concerned with realities) and *sacred* (because it is the work of the Supernaturals; (3) that myth is always related to a 'creation,' it tells how something came into existence, or how a pattern of behavior, an institution, a manner of working were established; this is why myths constitute the paradigms for all significant human acts; (4) that by knowing the myth one knows the 'origin' of thing and hence can control and manipulate them at will; this is not an 'external,' 'abstract' knowledge but a knowledge that one 'experiences' ritually, either by ceremonially recounting the myth or by performing the ritual for which it is the justification; (5) that in one way or another one 'lives' the myth, in the sense that one is seized by the sacred, exalting power of the events recollected or re-enacted." (Eliade, Mircea. Myth and Reality. Harper & Row, 1963, 18-19)

The rituals of technology, like the rituals practiced by archaic societies, are based on the premise that reality is universally deterministic in its meaning, conceptually complete and nomologically immutable, therefore predictable and controllable, which is logically inconsistent with the meaning-augmenting effect of Theory (or Myth) and necessitates its refutation and technological failure, disintegration, with future liabilities. Due to this ontological contradiction, technology is committed to enforcing a mythical reality that continuously loses its meaning, whereas reflexive consciousness creates a world in which meaning is universally consistent, integrated, despite its essential incompleteness.

If our world is unknowable on the basis of subjective experience then what kind of information is signified by the expression 'the world as we know it'? I suggest that the world is a language, a natural object-language that is conceptually integrated with our sense of embodiment and whose terms signify the types of functions and patterns we identify as 'experience'. This language is essentially incomplete but functionally consistent, held together by the laws of sense; not something we 'know' to be true but something we 'do with one another', reciprocally validate according to the consistency of one another's account of experience. The 'world as we know it' is the medium of socially mediated subjectivity that is continually augmented by reflexive, communicative action. Perhaps this is the crucial distinction between 'naive' nature and 'mythical' technology: nature is the functionally sufficient medium of consciousness, energetically free, self-sustaining, whereas technology is self-negating, self-terminating, not integrable, and must be intentionally energised as a ritual in order to be anything at all.

www.ingramcontent.com/pod-product-compliance
Lightning Source LLC
Chambersburg PA
CBHW040732220426
43209CB00087B/1597